Fiscally Informed Total Force Manpower

T0302756

Harry J. Thie, John Christian, Matthew Stafford,
Roland J. Yardley, Peter Schirmer

Prepared for the Office of the Secretary of Defense
Approved for public release; distribution unlimited

RAND NATIONAL DEFENSE RESEARCH INSTITUTE

This research was sponsored by the Office of the Secretary of Defense and conducted within the Forces and Resources Policy Center of the RAND National Defense Research Institute, a federally funded research and development center sponsored by the Office of the Secretary of Defense, the Joint Staff, the Unified Combatant Commands, the Department of the Navy, the Marine Corps, the defense agencies, and the defense Intelligence Community under Contract W74V8H-06-C-0002.

Library of Congress Cataloging-in-Publication Data is available for this publication.

ISBN 978-0-8330-4418-1

Published 2008 by the RAND Corporation
1776 Main Street, P.O. Box 2138, Santa Monica, CA 90407-2138
1200 South Hayes Street, Arlington, VA 22202-5050
4570 Fifth Avenue, Suite 600, Pittsburgh, PA 15213-2665
RAND URL: http://www.rand.org/
To order RAND documents or to obtain additional information, contact
Distribution Services: Telephone: (310) 451-7002;
Fax: (310) 451-6915; Email: order@rand.org

Preface

The RAND National Defense Research Institute was asked to review studies performed by internal and external organizations that have suggested methods for making fiscally informed manpower determinations. The research reported here is intended to be a short-term review of publicly available studies done within particular organizations or functional personnel communities. This monograph should be of interest to those concerned with military manpower requirements.

This research was sponsored by the Office of the Secretary of Defense and conducted within the Forces and Resources Policy Center of the RAND National Defense Research Institute, a federally funded research and development center sponsored by the Office of the Secretary of Defense, the Joint Staff, the Unified Combatant Commands, the Department of the Navy, the Marine Corps, the defense agencies, and the defense Intelligence Community.

For more information on RAND's Forces and Resources Policy Center, contact the Director, James Hosek. He can be reached by email at James_Hosek@rand.org; by phone at 310-393-0411, extension 7183; or by mail at the RAND Corporation, 1776 Main Street, Santa Monica, California 90407-2138. More information about RAND is available at www.rand.org.

Contents

Figures

Tables

Summary

This monograph communicates the results of a short-term review of how selected Department of Defense (DoD) components currently review and analyze manpower needs in particular organizations or personnel communities. We reviewed published material and conducted interviews to ascertain useful methods that might be used more widely. The research is not designed to be comprehensive or to review routine Service manpower determination methods. Instead, we are particularly interested in practices that are currently being used by DoD organizations that have yielded specific results.

Manpower Requirements

Manpower policy has existed in nearly its present form for more than 50 years. A number of findings emerge from a reading of the past half-century of manpower requirements studies:

- Manpower cost is a consideration across all time periods, but there appears to be more emphasis on the cost-effectiveness and labor productivity of manpower in recent years.
- In the early years of the Cold War, there was an emphasis on manpower requirements as they support major weapon systems; this evolved from an emphasis on specific weapon systems to more emphasis on the strategic and operational imperatives of the Services in general.

- References to "total force" approaches to manpower requirements began to appear in the 1970s and increased in prevalence after that.
- Very few studies during times of conflict have been motivated by manpower requirements.
- Rigorous, analytical modeling approaches to manpower requirements determination appear to be prevalent across all time periods.

DoD Provides Guidance for Manpower Planning

DoD provides guidance to manpower planners for decisions as to the type of workers needed to accomplish different tasks within DoD. This guidance maintains an emphasis on fiscally informed manpower decisions.[1] Specifically, it states the following:

- Manpower requirements are driven by workload and shall be established at the minimum levels necessary to accomplish mission and performance objectives.
- Assigned missions shall be accomplished using the least costly mix of personnel (military, civilian, and contract) consistent with military requirements and other needs of the department.
- Military (active and reserve) and civilian manpower resources shall be programmed in accordance with validated manpower requirements and within fiscal limits and acceptable levels of risk identified in DoD planning and programming guidance.

In 2006, DoD issued an implementing policy for determining the appropriate mix of manpower (military and civilian) and private-sector support necessary to accomplish DoD's missions.[2] The guidance states the following:

---

[1] DoD, Department of Defense Directive 1100.4, *Guidance for Manpower Management*, Washington, D.C.: U.S. Government Printing Office, February 12, 2005.

[2] DoD, Department of Defense Instruction 1100.22, *Guidance for Determining Workforce Mix*, Washington, D.C.: U.S. Government Printing Office, September 7, 2006a.

- When assessing manpower costs, manpower authorities shall not assume that military performance is less costly than either DoD civilian or contract performance.
- Economic analyses similar to those required by A-76 studies shall be conducted to justify use of military personnel.[3]
- Manpower authorities shall not designate manpower for military performance assuming that DoD civilian employees cannot be recruited or will not deploy to perform critical activities during peacetime or war.
- Manpower authorities shall consult personnel officials to verify whether DoD civilian employees are available or can be recruited and trained to perform the work. Additionally, manpower designations should reflect required work and not temporary assignments.

Taxonomy of Studies

A wide range of study types exists. We created a taxonomy of manpower requirements studies to characterize the 27 studies we reviewed (see Table S.1).

Observations from the Reviewed Studies and Interviews

Most of the studies we reviewed were prescriptive in that they suggest improvements to manpower requirements processes. Experts assert best practices in manpower requirements-setting and recommend analytically rigorous practices. However, there is little evidence presented in these reports that the recommendations were ever implemented. Moreover, the vast majority were done by a party external to the organization being studied. We believe that many internal studies are done but

---

[3] *Circular A-76*, published by the Office of Management and Budget, establishes federal policy regarding commercial-sector performance of a government-operated commercial activity.

Table S.1
Summary of Studies Reviewed

Aspect	Number of Studies	Description
Fiscally informed (FI)	18	Studies base their findings and recommendations on fiscal information.
Functional	12	Studies focus on one function across several departments.
Organizational	8	Studies focus on one organization with several functions.
Occupational	5	Studies focus on particular functions that each department possesses.
Service	16	Studies focus primarily on one Service.
Descriptive	11	Studies describe current methods for determining manpower requirements.
Prescriptive	23	Studies prescribe methods by which manpower determinations might be improved.
Integrative	9	Studies break the subjects down, describing and prescribing methods for each component.
External	26	Studies performed by a party external to the subject organization.
Internal	1	Studies performed by a party internal to the subject organization.

are not documented in a public or readily accessible form. Our interviews suggest that such studies tend to be implemented because they were chartered and followed by the most senior decisionmakers in the organization and had specific goals associated with them.

The studies we reviewed addressed such topics as the mission of the organization, its operating environment, the resources available, and the processes used. With respect to resources, a major theme in many of the studies is trading one resource for another—e.g., active manpower for reserve manpower, officers for enlisted, manpower for technology, or strength for experience.

Although many of the studies were "fiscally informed," we observed at least five different views of what that term means. Each of these views emphasizes cost or effectiveness somewhat differently. The views include cutting a workforce, trading one workforce for another, reinvesting fixed manpower in higher-valued functions, trading end-strength for experience, and making short-term technology investments to reduce manpower in the long term. Many variations of these views exist.

We also observed that "what counts" and "how to count" varies widely across the studies we reviewed. For example, some studies count end-strength, some man-years, and some operating strength; others convert strength counts for military and civilian personnel into dollar figures. In terms of how to count, studies run the gamut from economic cost to program/budget cost, with multiple variations to deal with cost savings versus cost avoidance, life cycle versus acquisition, investment versus operating and support, and standard programming rates versus grade- or occupation-specific rates.

Tradeoffs

Given the manpower guidance and the emphasis in studies on tradeoffs, we examined data that covered the 50 years of manpower guidance for evidence of desirable tradeoffs. Has the manpower equation moved toward "total force, fiscally informed" decisionmaking over a long period of time?

If we make the assertion that the military of 2005 is more capable and effective than the military of 1955, we could argue that its costs are down through greater use of DoD civilians and selected reserve than active military and through a smaller but more-experienced force. Using proportionally more officers than enlisted personnel and more technically qualified enlisted personnel (resulting in higher training costs) apparently leads to higher costs but also greater capability. One could also argue that the increased per-capita spending on contracts for hard goods and services allowed for military personnel reductions and thus decreased cost. Possibly the most significant manpower change that affected cost during the 50-year period is the halving of the size of the force from 1955 and an even greater reduction from the peak of the Vietnam era.

Conclusions

We were asked to review a number of manpower requirements studies to see whether there were particular methods that other organizations could replicate to help them make fiscally informed manpower decisions. Many methods were suggested in the studies we reviewed. Moreover, external evaluators typically use their own proprietary methods. Our interviews led us to conclude that a number of internal manpower requirements studies are done by organizations but are not publicly available. The published studies seldom show implementation; the internal studies described to us appear to have implementation as an attribute. Our judgment from this limited sample is that the method used for manpower requirements determination may not be as important as other attributes of the studies, such as the following:

- *The direct involvement of a senior decisionmaker in chartering, periodically reviewing, and deciding.* Manpower requirements change over time, and changes in mission or technological improvements (among other reasons) dictate a periodic review. Senior-level action and involvement show organizational emphasis and a scrutinized process to evaluate tradeoffs to meet mission requirements within fiscal constraints.
- *Specific stated goals as part of the study charter, using particular views of fiscally informed of the type outlined.* Reinvesting (rebalancing), trading one workforce for another, trading experience for strength, and investing in technology are different views that can lead to desirable outcomes; studies should be clear about goals as a basis for evaluation. Only with clearly stated goals can the tradeoffs of the goals be assessed and measured.
- *A holistic approach that considers organizational mission, environment, resources (past, present, future), and processes.* Our analysis revealed that many manpower study recommendations were not implemented. We do not know why is so, but perhaps unseen or unintended consequences would have resulted if the study recommendations had been implemented. A holistic view of the entire organization is necessary to understand the effect of how changes

in one area affect another area's mission, environment, resources, and processes presently and in the future.
- *Publicly available and auditable results.* This criterion allows for accountability and the measurement of the implemented results.
- *Methodology-based (the study can be replicated) but the methods may vary.* A clear set of measurement criteria must be established upon which decisions are made. This allows an activity to be measured against its stated goals.

We also found that there was no one "best" method; just taking action and making a decision also works. There were several instances of undocumented work that produced desired results.

In the future, those conducting manpower requirements studies are likely to ensure higher quality by striving to meet the attributes above.

Acknowledgments

Many individuals helped us to understand how the services and the Office of the Secretary of Defense view manpower requirements and studies that have been done to determine or review them. Our sponsor, Richard G. Robbins, was particularly helpful in identifying people to interview and studies to review. RAND colleagues Eric Larson and John Crown provided thoughtful reviews that improved this report.

Abbreviations

AC	active component
ANOVA	analysis of variance
AVF	all volunteer force
BUR	Bottom-Up Review
CBO	Congressional Budget Office
CINCLANTFLT	Commander In Chief, Atlantic Fleet (USN 2nd Fleet)
DARPA	Defense Advanced Research Projects Agency
DHP	Defense Health Program
DMC	Defense Mission Category
DMRR	Defense Manpower Requirements Report
DoD	Department of Defense
DPPC	Defense Planning and Programming Category
FI	fiscally informed
FFRDC	federally funded research and development center
FNMOC	Fleet Numerical Meteorology and Oceanography Center

FYDP	Future Years Defense Program
GAO	U.S. Government Accountability Office
IMA	Intermediate Maintenance Activity
LCS	Littoral Combat Ship
M&P IWAR	Manpower and Personnel Integrated Warfare Architecture
MEO	Most Efficient Organization
NAVO	Naval Oceanographic Office
NAVSO	United States Navy Forces, Southern Command
NCCA	Naval Center for Cost Analysis
O&S	operations and support
OJT	on-the-job training
OLS	ordinary least squares
OSD	Office of the Secretary of Defense
POF	Part of Force
PWS	Performance Work Statement
QDR	Quadrennial Defense Review
RC	reserve component
TDA	table of distribution
TFM	Total Force Management
VAMOSC	Visibility and Management of Operating and Support Costs
YOS	years of service

CHAPTER ONE

Introduction

The Department of Defense (DoD) is operating at a time when it must carefully balance resources to recapitalize major equipment—all while mitigating operational risk. DoD is carefully examining its discretionary resources to accomplish this task. One such resource that is being closely examined is the DoD workforce.

The initial manpower guidance for the DoD was published in 1954 and was not modified for 50 years. Prior to 1954, approaches to manpower determination could best be described as heuristics. For example, in the early 1900s, the Navy used a manpower equation based on ship tonnage (100 enlisted and five officers per 1,000 tons). This "personnel by the pound" method can be traced to manpower levels for ship classes up through the 1970s. Once the number of capital ships and the supporting fleet was determined, the manpower component was largely derivable. In World War I, General John J. Pershing and the French figured out ground manpower requirements based on how many divisions would be used. After that war, the Army continued to use the division metric to size the manpower requirement, shifting about four years ago to a brigade metric. When the Air Force emerged as a separate Service, its manpower requirement was structured around the number of airplanes.[1] Other militaries have used methods ranging from traditional means to specific manpower goals as a materiel design consideration. Over the years, many reports and studies, in particular those of the U.S. Government Accountability Office (GAO), have

[1] Sheila Nataraj Kirby and Harry J. Thie, *Enlisted Force Management: A Historical Perspective*, Santa Monica, Calif.: RAND Corporation, MR-755-OSD, 1996.

questioned the methods used for manpower determination.[2] Since the all-volunteer force (AVF) began, especially in the late 1990s and early 2000s, there has been a greater realization that military manpower is not free.[3] More recently, many militaries have emphasized the concept of life-cycle cost by attempting to balance acquisition cost with operating costs over the life cycle of a system. Most recently, emphases on capabilities, competencies, and human capital strategy have created additional focus on manpower determination and management. These advances in capabilities also make many legacy manpower demands obsolete.

Ideally, the DoD components should plan for Total Force[4] workforces that enable key capabilities, deliver readiness, are cost-effective, and balance risk. Demand exists both in the military and in the private sector for those who are trained and skilled to work with new and advanced technologies. DoD leadership must ensure that the processes governing the demand for people are agile, dynamic, and forward-looking and that the resulting demands are well-reasoned and fiscally informed, providing a balance between risk and readiness. Constrained resources means that workforce demand must be critically and objectively derived and challenged, and choices must be made. DoD must not spend more than is necessary to match the capability levels and associated degrees of risk the leadership is willing to accept.

---

[2] See for example, Defense Manpower Commission, *Defense Manpower: The Keystone to National Security, Report to the President and the Congress*, Washington, D.C., April 1976; GAO, *Military Officers: Assessment of the 1988 Defense Officer Requirements Study,* Washington, D.C.: U.S. Government Accountability Office, GAO/NSIAD-88-146, April 1988; GAO, *DoD Manpower: Information on the Accuracy of Defense Manpower Requirements*, Washington, D.C.: U.S. Government Accountability Office, GAO/NSAID-86-87BR, March 26, 1986a; and GAO, *Navy Manpower: Improved Ship Manpower Document Program Could Reduce Requirements*, Washington, D.C.: U.S. Government Acountability Office, NSIAD-86-49, March 27, 1986b.

[3] There are two threads to this realization. First, the cost of military manpower has risen significantly since the use of market wages after conscription ended in 1973, especially after the pay raises of 1980–1981. Also, military manpower is centrally budgeted and paid, so the user bears none of the direct cost.

[4] The Total Force is made up of active and reserve (including national guard) military manpower and DoD civilians. More recently, contractors have been included.

This Study

The RAND National Defense Research Institute was asked to undertake a brief review of published reports to ascertain good practices and processes currently used by DoD components to make fiscally informed workforce decisions such that other components might benefit from this knowledge. This review is also designed to consider the net effect of workforce planning within the broader context of defense planning and management, specifically delineating recommendations that would assist components in achieving the desired outcomes of DoD's senior leadership.

The purpose of this document is to communicate the results of a short-term review of how selected DoD components currently review and analyze manpower needs in particular organizations or personnel communities. We reviewed published material and conducted interviews to ascertain useful methods that might be used more widely.

This monograph examines current approaches to reviewing and analyzing workforce demand in particular organizations or personnel communities. The research is not designed to be comprehensive or to review routine Service manpower determination methods.[5] We review existing documentation, studies, and analyses done by federally funded research and development centers (FFRDCs), DoD components, other governmental agencies, and outside organizations to enumerate and describe practices and methods advocated for, or used by, DoD components and organizations. Of particular interest are practices that are currently being used by DoD organizations that have yielded specific results. The emphasis is not on purely military units or the process for generating military units. Instead, we emphasize practices and methods for requirements in the military or civilian personnel community or in

---

[5] Each Service has directives, regulations, and instructions that detail its established manpower methodologies. Subordinate Service organizations have adopted specific manpower methods. For example, Rakoff reported on an Army-Navy workforce planning demonstration symposium that highlighted Army and Navy workforce planning systems currently in use in those Services. See Stuart H. Rakoff, *Report on Army-Navy Workforce Planning Demonstration Symposium*, presented at 6th Annual Navy Workforce Research Conference, March 26, 2006.

organizations that include military, civilian employees, and contractors. We describe practices and methods that include results achieved, if known. Interviews were conducted selectively to improve description of practices.

In sum, our approach was to identify and collect publicly available studies, review the studies to generate a taxonomy for classifying them, code the studies according to the taxonomy, and analyze the results.

Organization of This Monograph

Following this introductory chapter, Chapter Two broadly reviews the changing emphases of manpower determination over the past 50 years. The third chapter describes the documentation, studies, and analyses that we reviewed. It includes the taxonomy we used to classify studies. (Details about the studies are in an appendix.) Chapter Four provides our initial observations based on our review. Chapter Five uses the data to assess results achieved in manpower use over 50 years. Chapter Six provides our conclusions, including our assessment of the attributes of a "useful" manpower study.

CHAPTER TWO

Manpower Requirements: Then to Now

Historical Trends in Manpower Requirements Studies

The primary focus of this monograph is on current and recent research related to fiscally informed Total Force manpower requirements. However, a brief summary of the history of this research can provide perspective on the ways in which the U.S. military's approach to manpower requirements has changed over time, reflecting the conditions of a particular time. Such a perspective can hopefully inform current policymaking, as decisionmakers face similar issues in the current day. This section reviews some of the historical trends in manpower requirements studies, with a particular emphasis on the RAND database of publications on the subject.[1]

A number of findings emerge from a reading of the past half-century of manpower requirements studies:

- Manpower cost is a consideration across all time periods, but there appears to be more emphasis on the cost-effectiveness and labor productivity of manpower in recent years.
- In the early years of the Cold War, there was an emphasis on manpower requirements as they support major weapon systems; this evolved from an emphasis on specific weapon systems to more

[1] Our emphasis on RAND studies is based partly on their preponderance and convenience. However, the pioneering work in this field began in the post–World War II period, as issues of military policy and organization began to be addressed in earnest using management and social science techniques. Research organizations, such as RAND, the Institute for Defense Analyses, and the Center for Naval Analyses, appear to be the best repositories of this work.

emphasis on the strategic and operational imperatives of the Services in general.
- References to "total force" approaches to manpower requirements begin to appear in the 1970s and increase in prevalence after that.
- Very few studies during times of conflict have manpower requirements as their motivating issue.[2]
- Rigorous, analytical modeling approaches to manpower requirements determination appear to be prevalent across time periods.

As mentioned elsewhere in this monograph, analyses of manpower requirements and manpower costs do not always coincide in the same research papers. However, our review of past studies shows that the cost of military personnel has been a continuous concern of policymakers. There appears to be a slight upward trend in this concern over time as the advent of the smaller AVF heightened awareness of the need for greater returns on investment to manpower. In earlier years, manpower was treated as a highly elastic resource in support of the major strategic weapon platforms of the day. For example, some Cold War–era RAND studies of manpower requirements had platform-specific titles. Over time, these studies yielded to broader investigations of the manpower requirements of entire occupations, functions, and other military communities. They all had in common an orientation toward the strategic mission and objectives of their respective components.

The concept of "total force" approaches to manpower requirements surfaces roughly around the time of the conversion to the AVF. For example, in 1974, RAND undertook a number of studies related to Air Force reservists, total force planning, and personnel costs.[3] Requirements studies increasingly referred to total force manpower over time,

---

[2] The Vietnam War, for example, figures in few manpower requirements studies from that era.

[3] Bernard Rostker, *Air Reserve Forces Personnel Study*, Vol. I: *The Personnel Structure and Posture of the Air National Guard and the Air Force Reserve,* Santa Monica, Calif.: RAND Corporation, R-1049-PR, 1973; Vol. III, *Total Force Planning, Personnel Costs, and the Supply of New Reservists*, Santa Monica, Calif.: RAND Corporation, R-1430-PR, 1974; F. J. Morgan, Leonard V. Scifers, and D. K. Shelton, *Air Reserve Forces Personnel Study,* Vol. IV: *Personnel*

substituting among active, reserve, and civilian personnel in various roles. This form of labor substitution requires greater knowledge of cost comparisons among the different types of personnel, and the literature contains a growing body of research dedicated to understanding the fiscal implications of interchangeability.

Interestingly, very few requirements studies have been motivated by the demands of wartime mobilization and operations. Although many of the manpower requirements models used in these studies undoubtedly take peacetime and wartime into consideration, there is little to suggest that this distinction is the key driver of any of the studies.[4] One could argue that they all take into account the primary missions of their subject organizations and by extension are calibrated for the contingencies of conflicts that are relevant to their time periods. Still, it is noteworthy that actual operations—which have changed dramatically from the days of the Cold War to the current global war on terror—have not been the central concern of most manpower requirements studies.

Finally, rigorous analytical modeling approaches to manpower requirements have a longstanding place in the literature. The complexities of manning a force as large and diverse as the U.S. military have often required technically sophisticated analyses. Many of these models were employed long before technological advances in computing that would have aided their implementation. Yet as a matter of practice, depending on the Service, occupation, or organization in question, there are many heuristics and nonanalytical approaches in use to determine manpower requirements. For example, allocating ranks to units based on look-up tables is a widely used heuristic. Allocating officer billets based on tradition is a nonanalytical heuristic. While manpower in operational units tends to be centrally analyzed, manpower in nonoperational units—e.g., Navy shore units or Army Table of Distribu-

---

Shortages and Combat Capability, Santa Monica, Calif.: RAND Corporation, R-1459-PR, 1974.

[4] For a notable, recent counterexample, see Cori Rattelman, Robert Levy, Neil Carey, and Flora Tsui, *Wartime Medical Requirements: Profiles and Requirement Determination Process*, Alexandria, Va.: Center for Naval Analyses, CAB D0004694.A2, October 2001.

tion (TDA) units—is frequently based on command judgments. To some degree, a combination of modeling and "common sense" methods is probably warranted, but the research literature tends to focus on the analytics of these difficult problems.

Drivers of Manpower Requirements—Force Structure Reviews

Force structure reviews are major drivers of manpower and force structure decisions over time. The Base Force review (1990), the Bottom-Up Review (BUR) (1993), and the 1997, 2001, and 2006 Quadrennial Defense Reviews (QDRs) influenced important force structure and manpower decisions.[5] Following is a brief summary of these reviews and their impact on manpower.

The Base Force review provided a new military strategy and force structure for the post–Cold War era and set a floor for force reductions. The Base Force review's effort resulted in force reductions and modest changes to the allocation of resources among the Services. The effort realized reductions of 25 percent in the force structure and 20 percent in active manpower but had difficulty realizing the goal of a 20 percent reduction in the reserves. Civilian manpower was reduced at a greater rate than that of active or reserve component personnel—a greater reduction than had initially been planned.[6]

The BUR reviewed the nation's defense strategy, force structure, modernization, infrastructure, and foundations that were appropriate for the post–Cold War era. The force structure and manpower reductions led to a reduction in forces of roughly one-third, which was beyond the Base Force's planned 25 percent reduction (over the 1990 force levels).

---

5 Eric V. Larson, David T. Orletsky, and Kristin Leuschner, *Defense Planning in a Decade of Change: Lessons from the Base Force, Bottom-Up Review, and Quadrennial Defense Review*, Santa Monica, Calif.: RAND Corporation, MR-1387, 2001.

6 Les Aspin, *The Bottom-Up Review: Forces for a New Era*, Washington, D.C.: U.S. Government Printing Office, September 1993.

QDRs are designed to be comprehensive examinations of defense needs and to identify potential threats, strategy, force structure, readiness posture, military modernization programs, defense infrastructure, and other elements of the defense program.

The aim of the 1997 QDR was to preserve the critical combat capabilities of the U.S. military forces—"the tooth"—while reducing infrastructure and support activities—"the tail"—wherever prudent and possible.[7] The QDR's recommendations resulted in the military departments and the defense agencies reducing active military end-strength by 60,000 personnel, reserve end-strength by about 55,000, and civilian personnel by 80,000, which were small changes in the Services' active combat forces.

The 2001 QDR focused on a capabilities-based approach to address how an adversary might fight rather than specifically who the adversary might be or where a war might occur.[8] The construct called for a better accounting for force requirements that are driven by forward presence and rotational issues. This capability-based strategy required a reliance on the reserve component (RC) forces and directed a comprehensive review of the active and reserve mix, organization, priority missions, and associated resources.

The 2006 QDR addressed DoD's Human Capital Strategy, which focuses on developing the right mix of people and skills across the Total Force. The Human Capital Strategy is based on an in-depth study of the competencies that U.S. forces require and the performance standards to which they must be developed. The QDR guidance directed the military departments to map the competencies and performance that constitute their forces and to evaluate and improve personnel development processes to achieve those standards. Advancements, awards, and compensation may then be linked to an individual's performance as

---

[7] DoD, *Report of the Quadrennial Defense Review*, Washington, D.C.: U.S. Government Printing Office, May 1997.

[8] DoD, *Quadrennial Defense Review Report*, Washington, D.C.: U.S. Government Printing Office, September 30, 2001.

opposed to longevity or time in grade, to better align incentives with outputs and to reward excellence.[9]

Another source for historical perspective on military manpower requirements is DoD's Defense Manpower Requirements Report (DMRR). This report is required annually by Section 115a of Title 10, U.S. Code. (The DoD directive that outlines the report was first issued in August 1954, and is commonly referred to by its number, 1100.4.) The purpose of the report is to provide "guidance to be used by the Services in the preparation and administration of their manpower programs and will review such programs, military and civilian."[10] For this study, we reviewed the DMRR for fiscal years 1989, 1995, 1997, and 2001 to document any notable trends in manpower requirements management. The following sections present highlights of the changes.

1989 to 1995

- Added medical manpower requirements "annex" to report
- Explicitly mentioned meeting requirements of the Goldwater-Nichols Act of 1986 (P.L. 99-433)
- Shifted emphasis from Cold War footing to peacetime missions and operations
- More emphasis placed on the use of the RC in stabilization operations, peacekeeping, and the like
- Changed reporting from the use of Defense Planning and Programming Categories (DPPCs), which were function-based, to Defense Mission Categories (DMCs), which are more mission-based
- Explicitly mentioned the "bottom-up review" defense strategy
- Took into account the drawdown and separation incentives of the early 1990s, as well as the potential need to reinstate legal authority for such incentives.

---

[9] DoD, *Quadrennial Defense Review Report,* Washington, D.C.: U.S. Government Printing Office, February 6, 2006b.

[10] DoD, 2005.

1995 to 1997

- Explicitly mentioned that scenario planning involving a worldwide war with primarily European operations was no longer realistic and that more-recent developments, such as Operations Desert Shield and Desert Storm, changed the manpower requirements process
- Added narrative structure to the introduction concerning force reductions, streamlining initiatives, and reduced budget authority; each Service summarized with respect to these initiatives.

1997 to 2001

- Added report sections about manpower request justifications from the Military Departments and the cost of manpower
- Discussed force reductions and downsizing in much greater detail, with reference to the changing role of the military in the post–Cold War environment. Mentioned the reduction of the acquisition workforce, ongoing review of inherently governmental functions, and review of DoD-wide major headquarters activities
- Ventured into politics by criticizing end-strength floors enacted by Congress.

2001 to 2005

- Addressed initiatives of reductions in the acquisition workforce; review of inherently governmental functions and DoD-wide major headquarters and support activities
- Streamlining initiatives aimed to make the DoD work better at lower cost
- Temporarily increased manpower requirements due to the global war on terror. A permanent increase not deemed to be in the nation's best interest because of increasingly high costs of military personnel.

2006

- Alternatives to large, permanent end-strength increases sought
- Manpower initiatives implemented to increase operational capability while relieving stress on the force:
  - Rebalancing capability and manpower within active component (AC) and RC
  - Conversion of military billets to civilian performance
  - Modularizing the Army and realigning Service force structure
  - Technology insertion and "jointness."

2007

- Important that all Services define workload requirements to realize capabilities in a cost-efficient manner
- Funds needed for other capability enablers
- Manpower investments to complement platforms, weapons, maintenance, and training to deliver required capabilities
- Services to arrive at fiscally informed Total Force manpower solutions.

Table 2.1 summarizes the changes in budgeted end-strength for both the AC and RC that were proposed in each year's DMRR.

Table 2.1
Change in Strength

Budgeted End-Strength	FY 1989	FY 1995	FY 1997	FY 2001	FY 2005
AC	2,174,200	1,525,700	1,457,000	1,381,000	1,389,300
RC[a]	1,150,900	979,000	900,900	865,700	820,800
Civilian	1,075,400	831,800	749,500	671,600	661,200

[a] Includes Selected Reserve (reserve and National Guard), full-time active guard and reserve members, and individual mobilization augmentees.

DoD Provides Guidance for Manpower Planning

Workload demands in the DoD require workers with specific sets of skills and experience. In this regard and with fiscally informed manpower decisions in mind, DoD provides guidance to manpower planners to guide decisions as to the type of workers needed to accomplishdifferent tasks within DoD.[11] This guidance maintains an emphasis on fiscally informed manpower decisions. Specifically, it states the following:

- Manpower requirements are driven by workload and shall be established at the minimum levels necessary to accomplish mission and performance objectives.
- Assigned missions shall be accomplished using the least costly mix of personnel (military, civilian and contract) consistent with military requirements and other needs of the department.
- Military (active and reserve) and civilian manpower resources shall be programmed in accordance with validated manpower requirements and within fiscal limits and acceptable levels of risk identified in defense planning and programming guidance.

In 2006, DoD issued an implementing policy for determining the appropriate mix of manpower (military and civilian) and private-sector support necessary to accomplish defense missions.[12] The guidance states the following:

- When assessing manpower costs, manpower authorities shall not assume that military performance is less costly than either DoD civilian or contract performance.
- Economic analyses similar to those required by A-76 studies shall be conducted to justify use of military personnel.
- Manpower authorities shall not designate manpower for military performance assuming that DoD civilian employees cannot be recruited or will not deploy to perform critical activities during peacetime or war.

---

[11] DoD, 2005.

[12] DoD, 2006.

- Manpower authorities shall consult personnel officials to verify whether DoD civilian employees are available or can be recruited and trained to perform the work. Additionally, manpower designations should reflect required work and not temporary assignments.

In this chapter, we have broadly reviewed the changing emphases of manpower determination over the past 50 years and discussed the major reviews that drove manpower requirements. In the next chapter, we describe the studies that we reviewed and discuss the taxonomy we used to classify them.

CHAPTER THREE

Existing Documentation, Studies, and Analysis

Toward a Taxonomy of Manpower Requirements Studies

A review of publicly available manpower requirements studies reveals a wide range of study types. Some studies focus on a narrow aspect of the requirements determination process, such as a specific organization or function, whereas others take a broad approach, examining the manpower requirements process for the entire Navy, for example. Some studies read more like descriptive histories than prescriptive proposals. For these reasons, a taxonomy of manpower requirements studies can provide analysts and policymakers with a useful way of understanding and categorizing the types of reports that have been produced. We identified several points of differentiation among manpower studies to develop a straightforward categorization template. This section describes those points of differentiation and the way we applied the approach to the studies under review. (The appendix summarizes each of the studies we reviewed, including its categorization.)

The public disclosure of a manpower study is the first and most basic point of differentiation. The literature review that we conducted was obviously limited to those reports that have been made publicly available either by their authors or their sponsors and that are readily located through electronic and Web-based searches. Most military manpower studies of this type are not classified; however, the possibility remains that some research in this area is kept confidential for various reasons. Although a fair amount of the manpower requirements research performed for or by the military is likely to be in the public domain, we suspect that a sizable portion of that research has remained proprietary and private. A variety of motivations might be behind such "invisible" research: sensitive data, proprietary methodologies, a perceived lack of interest in the broader market, or even benign indifference to publication. Federal laws and guidelines about the disclosure of government documents make it possible to bring even the most hidden studies to light; however, a thorough search of the literature is not likely to uncover the entire universe of manpower requirements research. Furthermore, it is not clear whether there is a systematic bias to the research that is made public as opposed to the portion that remains private. For example, private or proprietary studies might be more prescriptive, specifics-oriented, and directed toward implementation than public research is; in this regard, they might be more akin to consulting reports and recommendations than the academic research published in journals or by think tanks.

The last statement raises the next set of differentiation points in our taxonomy. Studies can be descriptive, prescriptive, or a combination of the two approaches. *Descriptive* studies offer an account of past or current methods of determining manpower requirements. Their aim tends to be the documentation of complex or poorly understood manpower requirements processes. Descriptive studies often give an historical account of manpower determination methodologies or paint a picture of the status quo. They tend to be more qualitative in nature than other types of studies. Their usefulness lies in their ability to demonstrate traditional manpower approaches in use by the military. They do not venture into recommendations or propose reforms; those that do we classified as prescriptive studies. *Prescriptive* studies suggest improvements to manpower requirements processes. They are more directed at applied practices. Prescriptive studies are useful for finding what experts believe are best practices in manpower requirements setting. They tend to point to methodologies that are more analytically rigorous than traditional practices are. Most studies in our review—at least 23 of them—have a prescriptive element; only about 11 have a descriptive approach. Some studies combine both descriptive and prescriptive aspects; in a few cases, we identified them as *integrative* studies because they analyzed components of the manpower requirements process in detail from both historical and forward-looking points of view.[1] Ideally, a manpower requirements study will examine the current situation as well as recommend changes.

Another key distinction outlined in our taxonomy is the level or unit of analysis. The level of analysis is important for analysts and policymakers who wish to borrow concepts or methods from another study and generalize them. Studies are classified as the following:

- *Functional:* The study focuses on one function across several departments (for example, the medical function), e.g., what is the most efficient mix of military and civilian manpower?
- *Organizational:* The study focuses on a single organization, command, department, or unit with multiple functions (for example, Naval Sea Systems Command), e.g., how do contracted services affect the need for military manpower?
- *Occupational:* The study focuses on a single occupation or role (for example, chaplains), e.g., what is the best military grade allocation?
- *Service:* The study pertains primarily to one of the Services, e.g., what is the military manpower need given future years' force structure?

There is some overlap and ambiguity among these categories, but most studies have a primary level of analysis. Additionally, there might be other ways of categorizing the level of analysis—for example, by geographic location—but these were not prevalent in the studies we reviewed. Of the studies in this analysis, 12 had a functional focus,

---

[1] For example, see John C. Barry and Paul L. Gillikin, *Comparative Analysis of Navy and Marine Corps Planning, Programming, Budgeting, and Execution Systems from a Manpower Perspective*, Monterey, Calif.: Naval Postgraduate School, A195234, March 2005. This master's thesis addresses Marine Corps and Navy manpower requirements, budgeting, and planning processes using an organizational systems framework. It describes the Services' organizations (and processes, to a lesser extent) and prescribes changes and is technically an integrative study in this regard. However, it is not a detailed examination of the requirements process itself, nor does it address the issue of fiscally informed requirements determination. It is mainly a comparative organizational study.

eight had an organizational focus, five had an occupational focus, and 16 involved a single Service.[2]

The author of the study serves as another category in the taxonomy. Studies are categorized as either *internal* (conducted by the subject organization itself or internal to the military) or *external* (conducted by a party external to the subject organization or outside the military). With few exceptions, external parties (e.g., research organizations, government agencies, or private consultancies) have conducted most of the studies. This point reinforces the possibility, postulated previously, that there are internally conducted reviews of manpower processes that are not publicly available. The authorship category is relevant for understanding the potential incentives, motivations, and biases of the parties involved in the studies, as well as judging their knowledge of the subject matter.

The final—and perhaps most important—category in our taxonomy is whether the study is *fiscally informed*. That is, does the study base its findings and recommendations on fiscal information of some form? About 17 studies in our literature review took a fiscal approach to the analysis of manpower requirements processes. The degree to which manpower studies consider cost is highly variable, however. Many studies do not consider cost at all; they look to the strategy and mission and use algorithms to determine the number of military personnel required to meet those goals. These kinds of unconstrained manpower studies are common; some were excluded from the literature review for this reason.[3] Other studies make a more explicit accounting of the costs of military personnel in the process of determining requirements. These studies tend to deal more with the issue of personnel cost than with the parts of the requirements process itself, however. For example, there is a significant body of research about the relative costs of military personnel versus civilian DoD or outsourced civilian personnel, but

[2] These and all other categories in our taxonomy are not mutually exclusive; a study can focus solely on one military Service and be an occupational study as well, for example.

[3] We believed that including some fiscally uninformed studies was warranted in cases in which the study was particularly interesting or detailed in some other aspect of military manpower requirements determination.

very little of this research touches on manpower requirements determination. Mission readiness and operational imperatives drive manpower requirements on one side of the spectrum; budgetary pressures drive personnel inventory cost decisions on the other. These opposing forces are left to meet in an unstructured way, filling a vacuum where fiscally informed manpower requirements studies would be germane. "Fiscally informed" in this sense is left open to interpretation: Does it mean reducing manpower cost for the same productivity? Keeping manpower costs constant while increasing productivity? Or is it possible to reduce costs and increase productivity at the same time? In addition, there are many ways of accounting for cost, and each way might lead to a different conclusion. For example, the economic cost of military personnel is not necessarily the same as programmatic or budgetary cost. Also, a policy change might be budget neutral for the federal government as a whole but could have significant effects at the level of the Services. How an organization interprets "fiscally informed" (FI) may depend in part on what it can control. An organization may have little control over the size of its budget or the number of military personnel it has. Conversely, some senior decisionmakers may control budgets for other organizations but may have little control over those organizations' manpower mix. Table 3.1 summarizes the studies we reviewed using the taxonomy described here.

We discuss our initial observations of the reviewed studies in the next chapter, as well as our observations of the approaches taken with the studies we examined.

Table 3.1
Summary of Studies

Aspect	Number of Studies	Description
FI	18	Studies base their findings and recommendations on fiscal information.
Functional	12	Studies focus on one function across several departments.
Organizational	8	Studies focus on one organization with several functions.
Occupational	5	Studies focus on particular functions that each department possesses.
Service	16	Studies focus primarily on one Service.
Descriptive	11	Studies describe the current methods for determining manpower requirements.
Prescriptive	23	Studies prescribe methods by which manpower determinations might be improved.
Integrative	9	Studies break the subjects down, describing and prescribing methods for each component.
External	26	Studies were performed by a party external to the subject organization.
Internal	1	Studies were performed by a party internal to the subject organization.

CHAPTER FOUR

Observations

This chapter summarizes our observations based on the taxonomy in the previous chapter and the studies themselves.

Most Studies Are External

More than 95 percent (26 of 27) of the studies we reviewed were performed by a party external to or separate from the organization being studied. Use of external evaluators appears to be a good practice. For example, in a study dealing largely with "human systems integration analysis," the GAO suggested that the Navy conduct such assessments and analyses to optimize crew size using the Human Systems Integration Directorate.[1] Optimally, such an external evaluator would study an organization and its operating environment and consolidate contributions from several different perspectives within it. The participation of leaders from different levels and from lateral offices allows for the inclusion of perspectives that are normally not in the line of sight of any single internal office within the organization. For this reason, and to eliminate the conflicts and biases of self-examination, it stands to reason that the evaluator should be external to the organization being examined.

The evaluator's job would be to recommend adjustments to resources and procedures with the aim of balancing the requirements

---

[1] GAO, *Military Personnel: Navy Actions Needed to Optimize Ship Crew Size and Reduce Total Ownership Costs*, Washington, D.C.: GAO, GAO-03-520, June 2003, p. 28.

of the mission and the environment at the lowest overall cost. External parties conducted nearly all the studies we read. Several specifically recommended that the subject organization "charge an agent or organization" external to the subject organization to conduct this kind of analysis in the future.[2]

Most Studies Are Prescriptive; Implementation Not Documented

More than 85 percent of the studies (23 of 27) prescribed methods for improving manpower determinations. Few of these studies presented evidence that the prescribed methods had been implemented in a fiscally informed way or in any way at all.

Suggesting a better method does not necessarily lead to implementation or use of the method for determining manpower. It may be that the "optimality" of the method may be less important than the actual use of any method (including heuristics) to arrive at fiscally informed manpower determinations. We discuss this further in Chapter Six.

Mission, Environment, Resources, and Processes: What to Study?

Among all the studies that we examined, the following variables stood out as the most often addressed:

- Mission of the organization
- Operating environment of the organization
- Resources available to the organization
- Processes used by the organization.

---

[2] Carol S. Moore et al., *Inside the Black Box: Assessing the Navy's Manpower Requirements Process*, Alexandria, Va.: Center for Naval Analyses, CRM-D0005206.A2, March 2002.

All the studies we reviewed took mission, environment, resources, and processes into account, even if not referring overtly to them as such. Some stood out because of the way in which they combined the resources and processes in their recommendations. Others stood out because of the way they accounted for the relationship between mission and environment. *Wartime Medical Requirements: Profiles and Requirement Determination Processes*[3] specifically evaluates the Naval medical establishment's capacity to adapt its resources and processes to fit changes to its environment and mission from peacetime to wartime. The authors of *Developing Cost-Effectiveness Guidelines for Managing Personnel Resources in a Total Force Context* call similar attention to operational environment, saying that

> [e]ven if using civilians is less costly than using active personnel and even if civilians are fully available for wartime work, costs may nevertheless be saved by replacing some civilians with actives under a mobilization program.[4]

The idea of trading one resource for another is a major theme in at least eight of the studies we examined. Most of those eight concern themselves primarily with tradeoffs and balances between military and civilian personnel. Some, however, balanced active against reserve,[5] and at least one considered saving by trading officers for enlisted personnel.[6] One in particular broached the idea of trading manpower requirements for technology—trading resource costs for a combination of resources

---

[3] Rattelman et al., 2001.

[4] C. Peter Rydell, Adele R. Palmer, and David J. Osbaldeston, *Developing Cost-Effectiveness Guidelines for Managing Personnel Resources in a Total Force Context*, Santa Monica, Calif.: RAND Corporation, R-4005/1-FMP, 1991.

[5] GAO, *Force Structure: Assessments of Navy Reserve Manpower Requirements Need to Consider the Most Cost-Effective Mix of Active and Reserve Manpower to Meet Mission Needs*, Washington, D.C.: U.S. Government Accountability Office, GAO-06-125, 2005b.

[6] Kenneth G. Harris, *Restructuring the United States Navy Chaplain Corps*, Monterey, Calif.: Naval Postgraduate School, September 2005.

and procedures, which is less expensive.[7] The authors explain that this has some potential, though it was limited in several of the cases they examined. Another set of studies, represented by Horowitz, suggests trading experience for numbers.[8]

Some studies directly address the relationships among resources, environment, and missions. For example, the GAO specifically states that "human capital shortfalls can threaten the agency's ability to perform its missions efficiently and effectively, especially when the environment has changed significantly."[9] In other reports, the authors make a point of building these variables into the main structure of their studies. For example, in *Inside the Black Box: Assessing the Navy's Manpower Requirements Process,*[10] the authors lay out the four objectives of their study. The first is to find whether it is "possible to reduce manning while maintaining operational standards"; it discusses technological substitutions and crews with more skill. The second objective is to find what a requirements process can achieve and whether the Navy's business practices undermine those processes. This question deals with whether current practices conflict with a potentially more efficient requirements process. The third objective asks what determines requirements and whether those factors should drive requirements. This deals with the connections between missions and the procedures. Finally, their fourth objective asks what the Navy could borrow from the private sector to incorporate efficiency into the Navy's system.

In *An Integrative Modeling Approach for Managing the Total Defense Labor Force*[11] and *Developing Cost-Effectiveness Guidelines for*

---

7 Karen D. Smith et al., *Is NAVSO Organized and Staffed to Do Its Job?* Alexandria, Va.: Center for Naval Analyses, CRM-D0005057.A1, January 2002.

8 Stanley A. Horowitz, *Skill Mix, Experience, and Readiness*, Alexandria, Va.: Center for Naval Analyses, October 1983.

9 GAO, *Military Personnel: DoD Needs to Conduct a Data-Driven Analysis of Active Military Personnel Levels Required to Implement the Defense Strategy*, Washington, D.C.: U.S. Government Accountability Office, GAO-05-200, 2005a, p. 2.

10 Moore et al., 2002.

11 Adele R. Palmer and C. Peter Rydell, *An Integrative Modeling Approach for Managing the Total Defense Labor Force*, Santa Monica, Calif.: RAND Corporation, R-3756-OSD/AF, December 1989.

Managing Personnel Resources in a Total Force Context,[12] the authors examine the "relationships between wartime and peacetime (types of environment) manpower roles and between military and civilian (types of resources) manpower utilization—and how can these relationships be integrated in a manpower management model [procedure]." The first report lists relationships between the variables and building the organization's required flexibility into the mission and addresses the implications for the operating environment. It further addresses the breadth of variety of missions, referred to as "wartime and peacetime capability goals," subsumed under the DoD. The goal of this report is to build a model that incorporates these characteristics, allowing for the balance we described earlier. In the second publication, the authors extend the model to make it applicable to other programs, such as retraining, mobilization, and rotation.

Multiple Views of Fiscally Informed, Total-Force Decisions Exist

As we reviewed studies and discussed them with study participants, we observed at least five different views of the term *fiscally informed.* Each of these views emphasizes cost or effectiveness somewhat differently.[13] For the most part, the focus of FI is lower cost, i.e., cost is first reduced and maintenance of, or reduction in, the amount of mission work (effectiveness) follows.[14] The five views are as follows:

---

[12] Rydell, Palmer, and Osbaldeston, 1991.

[13] A key assumption underlying these views is that individual daily work hours remain constant. Thus, if manpower costs are reduced by virtue of a smaller workforce, the workday does not expand to keep constant the amount of workforce output (effectiveness). Anecdotally, this happens, especially with a military workforce compared to private-sector workforce practices. In the military, the size of the workforce is fixed and, if work expands (or if the workforce contracts but the work does not), the duty day expands to accomplish the work. In the private sector, whether by law, contract, or practice, the length of the workday (week) is often fixed, and if work expands, it is accommodated through paid overtime, part-time (temporary) workers, or other workplace practices.

[14] In periods of mission growth, the opposite would be true. For example, end-strength increases in the USMC and U.S. Army should lead to greater effectiveness but higher cost.

1. *Cut the workforce to save dollars, especially the highest-cost workforce.* In this view, cost is reduced and effectiveness is arguably reduced as well, under the assumption that the workforce is contributing value to output. One could argue about the extent of the value compared to its cost. Program budget decisions (either formal or made internally to a Service or organization) are typical examples of this view.
2. *Trade one workforce for another.* In this view, cost is reduced, but effectiveness arguably stays the same. While the overall number of workers stays the same, under the assumption that the highest-cost workforce is being replaced, overall cost would go down. This is the logic that underlies decisions about replacing the military workforce with a civilian workforce. It is possible that, in certain specific situations, one might add the higher-cost workforce (typically, but not always, military) because of specific mission requirements.
3. *Reinvest fixed manpower resources in higher-value functional areas.* In this view, cost would stay the same, but effectiveness would increase. Examples include the functional rebalancing that some Services undertook in their military workforces to better prosecute the global war on terror.
4. *Trade end-strength for experience.* In other words, use a smaller but more-experienced workforce. In this view, cost would stay the same while effectiveness increased (or at worst stayed the same). Alternatively, cost could be reduced while effectiveness stayed the same. Variations of this view would include higher cost and higher effectiveness.
5. *Make a short-term investment to reduce manpower in the long term.* In this view, cost is increased, and effectiveness stays the same in the short term; in the long term, costs are reduced, and effectiveness stays the same. The short-term investment is exceeded by the net present (time) value of the long-term savings that produce the benefit. An example is an increased short-term materiel acquisition cost for technology that reduces the long-term life-cycle cost of manpower. A variant is to substi-

tute improved work practices for manpower that might more directly lead to lower cost at the same effectiveness.

These five views do not necessarily cover all possibilities. For example, recent increases in Army and Marine Corps end-strength presumably will increase capability as well. Table 4.1 contrasts the two issues of manpower effectiveness and manpower cost with each issue on one of the axes of the table. For each, we use a scale of increased, same, and decreased. The five views are placed in appropriate boxes and given a summary assessment. Other boxes are feasible and are labeled with likely or possible assessments.

Of the views outlined above, view 1 is undesirable but often necessary when the budget decreases but planned work has not. Eventually, less work gets done (decreased effectiveness). View 2 appears to be the one currently most associated with FI, in that many initiatives emphasize trading one workforce for another. View 3 is very beneficial at first look, given that an organization can take on higher-value functions while divesting (stopping performance of) lower-value functions.

View 4, in its purest form, is neutral in terms of desirability, because it could use different workforces with similar costs to pro-

Table 4.1
Assessment of Different Views of "Fiscally Informed"

		Manpower Capability		
		Increased	**Same**	**Decreased**
Manpower Cost	**Increased**	Acceptable?	View 5 (short-term) Path to long term?	Very undesirable
	Same	View 3 Beneficial	View 4 Neutral	Undesirable
	Decreased	Nirvana	Views 2, 4, 5 (long term) Current FI meaning?	View 1 Unavoidable?

duce comparable effectiveness. The proponents for the experience for strength tradeoff (view 4) would argue, however, that this approach eventually leads to decreased cost for similar effectiveness. View 5 is costlier in the short term but a reasonable path to a desirable long-term benefit. Thus, views 2, 4, and 5 all appear desirable over the long term.

Obviously, increased effectiveness with decreased cost is highly desirable but not easily achieved. Discussion with some subject-matter experts indicated that they have observed occurrences of this in the private sector. Typically, they cite reductions in management bureaucracy (at company headquarters, for example) that empower more productive operations. We found no specific examples of this reduction in the studies we reviewed.

In summary, while multiple views of FI exist, the emphasis of FI appears to be on decreasing manpower cost. Maintaining manpower effectiveness is desirable and achievable, but some would argue that reduced effectiveness is unavoidable if manpower is reduced.

"What Counts" and "How to Count" Are Not Specified

Different studies measure different aspects of the manpower equations and count them in different ways.

What Counts?

For military manpower, studies typically deal with head count or end-strength. However, some would argue that end-strength is a flawed measure and that man-years would be a better metric. Also, not all end-strength is the same—there are differences in "strength." Operating strength (end-strength that is allocated to such units as battalions, squadrons, or ships) has greater value than individuals' strength (end-strength that is allocated to account for transients, trainees, patients, and prisoners), because it shows the productive value of military manpower expeditures.

For DoD civilians and contractors, dollars count more than end-strength. However, DoD is attempting to convert the dollars allocated to contracts into a "head count" figure to gain an understanding of how many contractors are employed and where. Moreover, the issue of administrative head count versus dollar measures for the civilian workforce has been debated for years. Also, in addition to the end-strength count, military strength is also counted in dollars.

How to Count?

Let us count the ways:

- Economic cost versus program/budget cost
- Current year cost, budget year cost, Future Years Defense Program (FYDP) or program cost, or Congressional Budget Office (CBO) scoring cost (10-year)
- Cost savings versus cost avoidance
- Life-cycle cost versus acquisition cost
- Investment accounts versus operating and support accounts
- Standard programming rates versus grade- or occupation-specific rates
- Regular military compensation versus basic military compensation
- True "cost of a sailor" versus annual budget cost.

Although we believe this list to be representative of the range of ways in which one can count, it almost certainly is not exhaustive.

Undocumented Reviews Tend to Have Implementation

During our interviews, we learned of studies or analyses that had been performed and had led to implementation. Some of these studies dealt with particular organizations, and implementation was local and did not deal with large numbers (for example, Army headquarters). Other studies dealt with large functional areas (e.g., medical) or entire Services (e.g., Air Force). What these studies have in common is that all were either chartered by, supported by, or decided by the most senior people in the department or Service, and, according to our interviews, had been or were being implemented. However, these analyses are not documented in a public or in a readily accessible form. Some studies were done by external evaluators, and some were done internally. We believe that many internal studies are not documented and made publicly available, and we do not know whether the few described to us in interviews are representative of implementation for all of them.

In view of the initial observations of the reviewed studies and the various approaches taken to make fiscally informed manpower decisions, we turn in the next chapter to a data-based review to assess results achieved in manpower use over the past 50 years.

CHAPTER FIVE

Fifty Years of Manpower Tradeoffs: What Has Happened?

As stated previously, DoD manpower guidance has existed in its present form for slightly longer than 50 years. Significant policy changes (e.g., the AVF, Total Force policy) have occurred every 10 to 15 years over that time frame. But the basic guidance has been reasonably constant:

- Use minimum manpower to provide maximum effectiveness.
- Periodically evaluate policies, procedures, and structures.
- Maintain the lowest practicable level of manpower in support functions.
- Use the least-costly mix of personnel.

Manpower Tradeoffs

What has occurred with respect to manpower tradeoffs over this 50-year time frame? Multiple tradeoffs are discernible. We do not know whether these tradeoffs were caused by consistent application of policy or "just happened" over time. Moreover, the tradeoffs do not always appear to conform to guidance, but there may be good reasons for that. In the following figures, we examine multiple tradeoffs that have occurred, deliberate or not: civilian for military, reserve for active, experience for strength, officer for enlisted, senior for junior, contractor and capital equipment (technology) for DoD workforce, and specialists for generalists. The data shown are aggregated for all of DoD, and they mask individual Service differences that could, in fact, take different trends. We make the assertion that the military of 2005 is significantly more capable than that of 1955 and that this fact should be considered in assessing these apparent tradeoffs. The tradeoffs may not be the cause of the increase in capability, but one could at least argue for second- and third-order effects.

Figure 5.1 shows the ratio of selected reservists to active military. The higher the ratio, the more selected reservists are being used compared to active military. Shifts such as this, especially noticeable with Total Force policy, appear to conform to manpower guidance.

Figure 5.2 portrays a similar ratio for DoD civilian employees compared with the active military. Both figures appear to be implementations of DoD guidance to use civilian manpower before military manpower and RC manpower before AC manpower. Moreover, while ups and downs in these ratios are evident over different time periods, both are headed in the desired direction, although whether the rate of change is at a desirable pace is not known. The decrease in the civilian-to-military ratio since about 1995 appears to be reversing.

Figure 5.1
Ratio of Selected Reserve to Active Military

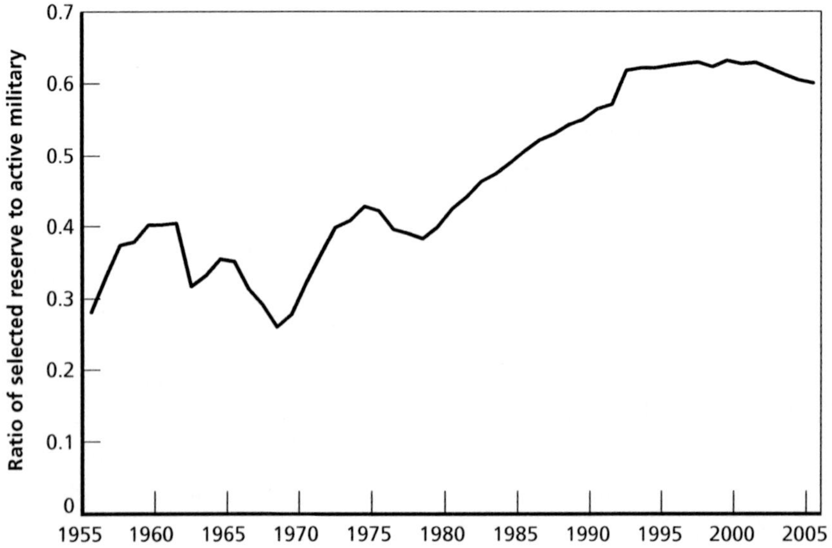

RAND *MG606-5.1*

Figure 5.2
Ratio of DoD Civilians to Active Military

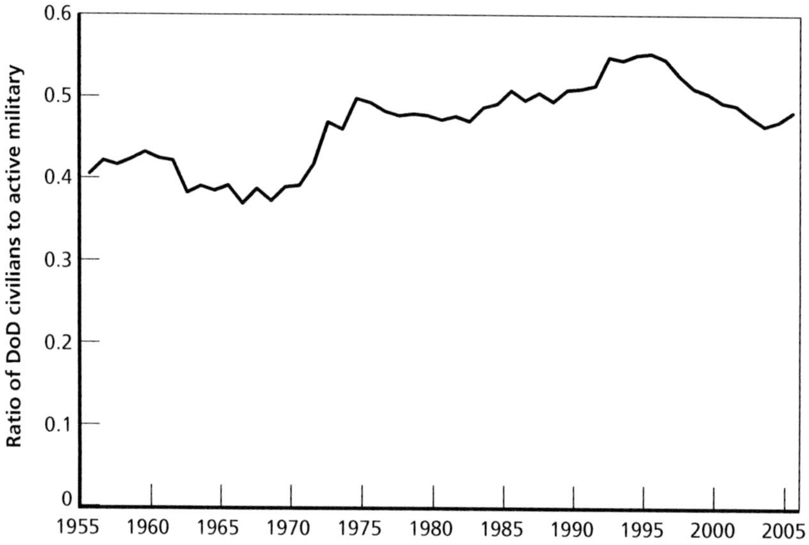

RAND *MG606-5.2*

This decrease in the ratio appears to be the result of cutting civilian manpower (view 1 in the previous chapter) rather than substituting civilian for military.

Figure 5.3 shows the ratio of enlisted personnel to officers, indicating a tradeoff within the active-duty military. On average, there are about five enlisted personnel for each officer, a ratio that has been decreasing for a number of years. Among the Services, the Marine Corps has the highest ratio and the Air Force the lowest, with the Army and Navy at about the overall average of five. This appears to be a case of substituting a higher-cost workforce for a lower-cost workforce, but we have no direct evidence as to what is driving this long-standing manpower trend (over 100 years).

Figure 5.4 portrays the relationship between end-strength and experience (as measured by years of service) for the period. Both strength and average years of service (YOS) are shown as percentages of their 2005 value. Strength in 1955 was about twice what it is now; average years of experience in 1955 were about half what they are now. There is a significant correlation between the two over the

Figure 5.3
Ratio of Active Component Enlisted Personnel to Officers

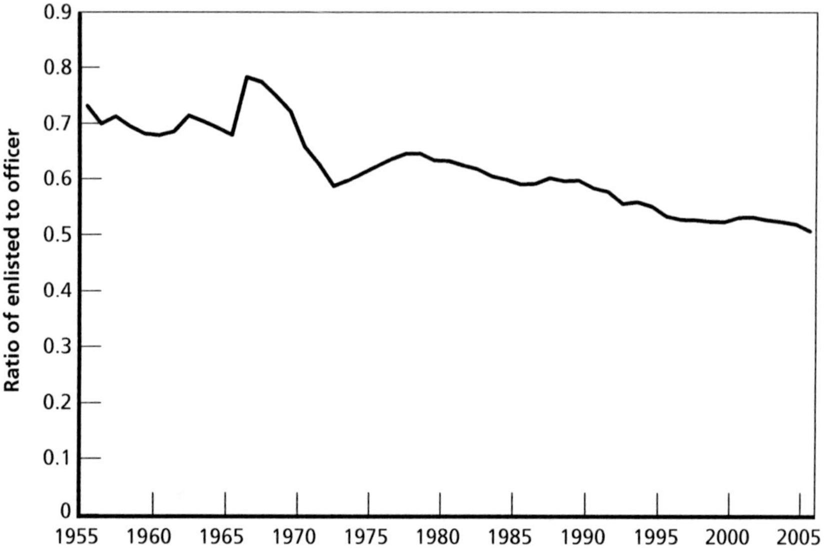

RAND *MG606-5.3*

50-year period: As experience doubled, strength halved.[1] The changes in strength and experience over that time were largely the effects of important structural changes. For example, strength increased significantly during the Vietnam War period, and—with short terms of service and high accessions—experience decreased. With the start of the AVF in the early 1970s, experience began to rise as the number of new entrants decreased with the reduction in strength and increase in initial terms of service. The 1980s saw retention and experience increase for a number of reasons, including pay increases. The drawdown of the 1990s was largely accomplished by reducing accessions, so experience continued to increase. Over the past ten years, strength and experience levels have stayed about the same. Cause and effect are not provable, but one could state as a fact that the more-capable military of today has fewer, but more-experienced, people than it had before.

---

1 The correlation is –0.87.

Figure 5.4
Relationship of End-Strength and Average Experience

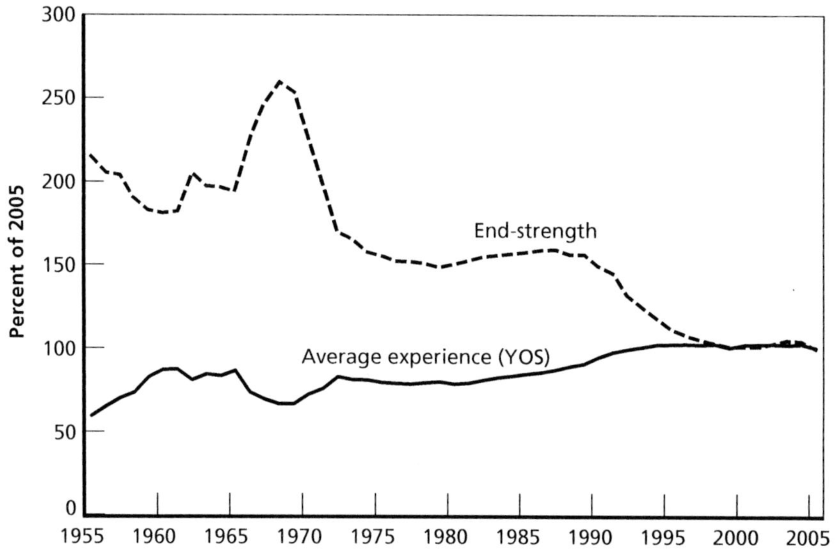

RAND *MG606-5.4*

Similarly, Figure 5.5 shows the relationship between senior enlisted personnel (the top five or the highest five enlisted grades) and junior enlisted personnel. The lines represent the share of the enlisted force. (The sum of the lines is 100 percent.) While the enlisted population was nearly 70 percent junior in 1958, it is currently nearly one-half junior and one-half senior.

Figure 5.6 shows the relationship between contract awards in the United States for hard goods (tanks, planes, ships, bullets) and services per active military person. (The prime contract awards are measured in FY 2000 dollars.) One could argue that significant investments in long-life technology (hard goods) have been made, as have annual purchases of labor substitution services contracts. The average active military person is supported annually by about $100,000 in new technology and services contracts.

Figure 5.5
Relationship of Senior and Junior Enlisted Personnel

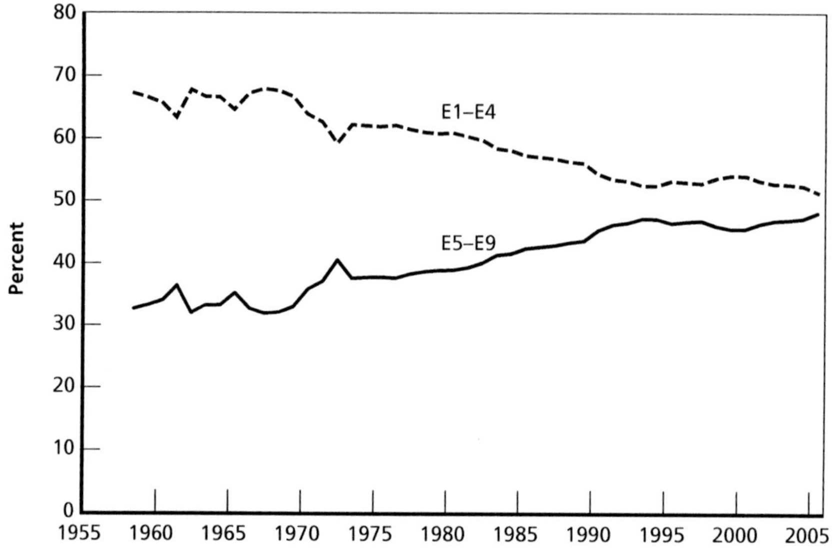

RAND *MG606-5.5*

Finally, Figure 5.7 shows the occupational tradeoff between enlisted specialists and generalists that has occurred throughout modern military history. The number of general military personnel (infantry, artillery, seamen) decreased as service and supply, clerical, craftsmen, and technical personnel contributed an increasing share to military and naval capability. This is somewhat misleading, because general military personnel in the U.S. military are themselves highly trained and use sophisticated technology. They are specialists in their own right. Significantly, the share of personnel devoted to service and supply, clerical, and mechanical maintenance functions in the AC appears to be decreasing. One could argue that the technical part of the military is shifting away from the mechanical to the electronic and medical, while clerical and supply is shifting to general military.

Figure 5.6
Ratio of Prime Contract Awards to Active Military Personnel

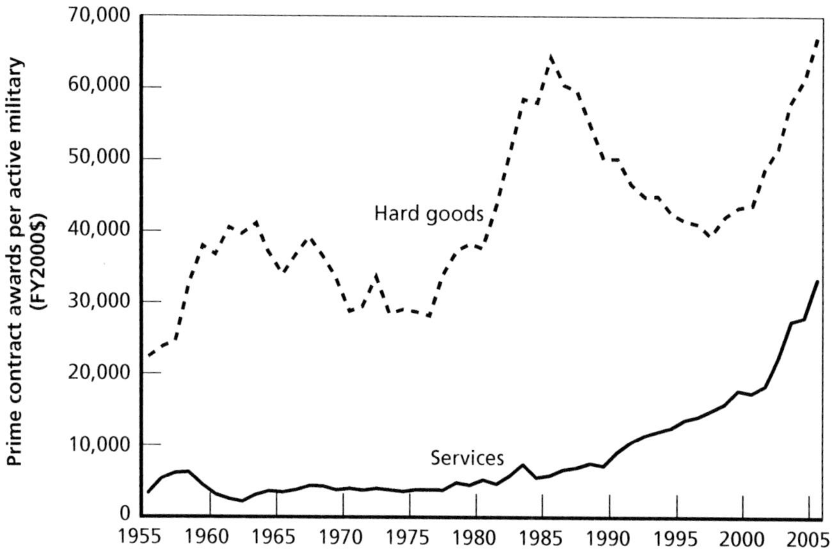

RAND *MG606-5.6*

Results of Tradeoffs Accumulate over Long Periods

Has the manpower equation moved toward "total force, fiscally informed" over a long period of time? If we reiterate the assertion that the military of 2005 is more capable and effective than the military of 1955, we could argue that its costs are down through greater use of DoD civilians and selected reserve than active military and possibly through a smaller but more-experienced enlisted force. Using proportionally more officers than enlisted and using more technically qualified personnel (higher training costs) would apparently lead to higher costs but also greater capability. One could argue that the increased per-capita spending on hard goods and services contracts either increased costs or allowed for military personnel reductions and thus decreased costs. Table 5.1 shows our assessment. We did not attempt to compute a net cost compared to the capability increase. Possibly the most significant

Figure 5.7
Occupational Distribution of the Enlisted Force

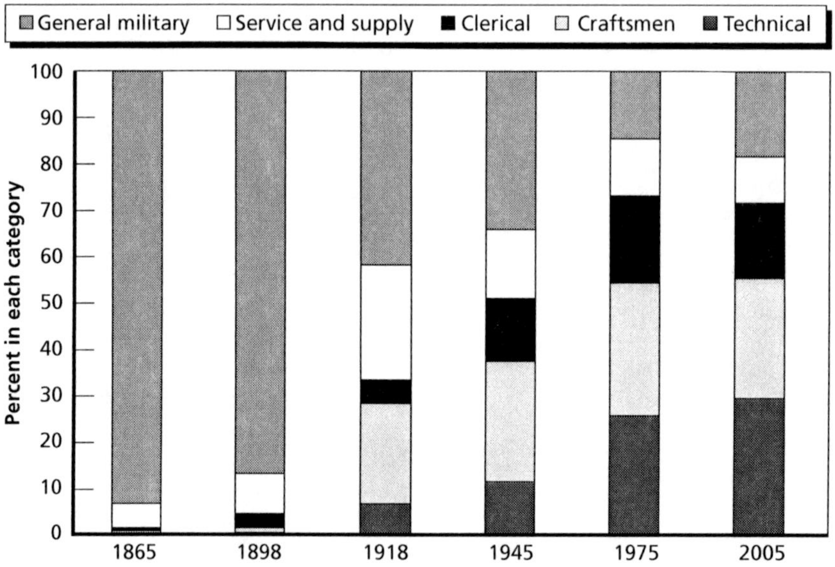

RAND *MG606-5.7*

Table 5.1
Assessment in Change in Cost for Various Manpower Tradeoffs

Manpower Tradeoff	Change in Cost
Proportionally more DoD civilians and selected reserve than active military	Less
Proportionally more officers than enlisted	More
Proportionally fewer, but more-experienced, enlisted	Less or same
Proportionally more technical occupations	More
More hard goods and services contracts	More or same
Smaller, but more capable, force	Less

manpower change is the halving of the size of the force from 1955 and an even greater reduction from the peak of the Vietnam conflict. At today's rates, a force of either size would add in excess of $100 billion to the annual military personnel costs and the defense budget.

We have broadly reviewed the changing emphases of manpower determination over the past 50 years and described the documentation, studies, and analyses that we reviewed. We provided our initial observations and presented a data-based assessment of results achieved in manpower use over 50 years. In the next chapter, we provide our conclusions to include our assessment of the attributes of a "useful" manpower study.

CHAPTER SIX

Conclusions

We were asked to review a number of studies to see whether they demonstrated methods that would be useful for other organizations in making fiscally informed manpower decisions. We did not ascertain one or more measures of "successful" or best studies. Instead, we observed studies that appeared useful in that they provided information and insights, allowed decisionmaking, and described tradeoffs. The success of these individual studies had to be defined by the person who chartered the study. Many methods were suggested in the studies we reviewed. Moreover, those who conduct external studies typically use proprietary methods. Our conclusion, based on all the studies we reviewed, is that the method used may not be as important to usefulness as other attributes of the studies—in particular, the direct involvement of a senior decisionmaker, which seems to be associated with actual implementation.

Other attributes we judged important to usefulness are the following:

- *Specific goals should be stated as part of the study charter, using particular views of fiscally informed of the type outlined.* Reinvesting (rebalancing), trading one workforce for another, trading experience for strength, and investing in technology are all views that can lead to desirable outcomes; studies should be clear about goals as a basis for evaluation. Only with clearly stated goals can the tradeoffs of the goals be assessed and measured.
- *A holistic approach must be taken that considers organizational mission, environment, resources (past, present, future), and processes.* We

do not know why many of the results of the studies that we examined were not implemented. Perhaps unseen or unintended consequences might have resulted if the study recommendations were implemented. A holistic view of the entire organization is necessary to understand how changes in one area may affect another area's mission, environment, resources, and processes—both in the present and in the future.

- *The results should be publicly available and auditable.* This criterion allows for accountability and the measurement of the implemented results.
- *The study should be methodology-based (so it can be replicated) but the methods may vary.* A clear set of criteria must be established against which to measure and on which decisions are made. This allows for measurement of an activity versus the stated goals.

Moreover, such studies should be undertaken routinely (periodically and on a time-driven schedule) and in response to mission and environmental changes (event-driven). Conducting studies on a regular basis captures accumulated changes in the operating environment. Changed missions should have resource implications.

In closing, our analyses of past fiscally informed manpower studies suggest a number of practices that should be encouraged in future studies.

APPENDIX

Studies

Wartime Medical Requirements: Profiles and Requirement Determination Processes

Authors: Cori Rattelman et al.
Publisher: Center for Naval Analyses
Date: October 2001

Purpose/Summary/Abstract

- Study objectives:
  - Describe how medical manpower requirements are determined.
  - Find out whether they can be met by the current fiscal year authorizations and the bodies that existed at the time of the survey.
  - Evaluate the impact on wartime medical requirements as a result of changes in the Defense Planning Guidance and other policy decisions.
- Study detailed the process from the force structure level down to wartime requirements determination.
- Fiscal aspects are wrapped into whether the requirements can be met with current authorizations as given in the billet file.

Methodological Approach

- Separated medical capability by platform and analyzed each individually (theater workload, force structure, then reserves).

- Starts off very generally, giving an overview of manpower determination in the Navy and then becoming more specific.
- Compares wartime requirement to billets authorized (by specialty, not platform), and then to personnel available.

Results and Recommendations

- Programming looks forward, but planning determines current needs.
- The programmer and the planner should confer more to determine requirements.
- The programming process is reasonable.
- Manpower determination process is hard to duplicate, especially for the fleet marine force.
- In general, billets and bodies can meet wartime requirements.
- Mismatches occur at the specialty level.
- Billet file is unreliable for wartime requirements.

DoD Manpower: Information on the Accuracy of Defense Manpower Requirements

Publisher: U.S. General Accounting Office
Date: March 26, 1986
For: Les Aspin, chairman of the U.S. House of Representatives Committee on the Armed Services

Purpose/Summary/Abstract

- This is a summary of a series of studies conducted on each of the armed Services. It details the GAO's findings on whether the Services' reporting and determination systems are accurate, becoming more accurate, or reporting deflated or inflated numbers; why there may be discrepancies, and briefly and generally how the Services may go about fixing these issues.

- The report focuses mainly on the armed Services as large entities and little on the DoD.
- Study often refers to fiscal considerations as impediments to appropriate manning requirements—e.g., "We found the process used to establish the manpower structure to be unsystematic and highly reactive to fiscal and manpower constraints."

Methodological Approach

- Critiqued methods and assumptions of Service manpower-determining institutions.
- Covered the Navy extensively, the Army somewhat, and the Marines briefly.
- Composed of several different studies previously conducted by the GAO.
- Includes examination of Table of Organization and Equipment (TO&E)–type units.
- May be especially useful as a reference tool for unofficial studies.

Results and Recommendations

- The report discussed problems with manning standards (equations relating manpower requirements to workload) several times.
- Internal determination machinery often relied on unrealistic assumptions; internal audit processes were performed by insufficiently trained personnel—or often not performed at all.
- Often, reviews were not performed, and Services failed to monitor effectively.
- Took issue with subjective determination methods, such as relying on what a battalion should look like and manning it from that point of view rather than from the requirements of the missions.
- Lack of adequate planning prior to the determination of manpower requirements.

Setting Requirements for Maintenance Manpower in the U.S. Air Force

Authors: Carl J. Dahlman, Robert Kerchner, and David E. Thaler
Publisher: RAND, Project AIR FORCE
Date: 2002
For: General Michael Ryan, Chief of Staff of the Air Force

Purpose/Summary/Abstract

- To review the methodology that the Air Force uses to determine active-duty enlisted manpower requirements in aircraft maintenance and to investigate whether there are any indications that these requirements—and the authorizations based on them—are underestimated.
- To identify the steps the Air Force can take to provide more complete information to its decisionmakers in their efforts to remedy shortfalls described.
- Briefly acknowledges the fiscal restraints imposed upon manpower but does not propose a determination method based on fiscal resources.

Methodological Approach

- Split the requirements for determining manpower requirements into three sections, each of which would represent the number of hours programmed or available to perform the activities associated with that section.
- The three sections are (1) hours derived from the Logistics Composite Manual (LCOM), (2) hours allowed by Major Command (MAJCOM)–wide standards away from primary duties, and (3) tasks that maintainers must accomplish during the remainder of the day but that are not represented in the other two sections.

Results and Recommendations

- Maintenance manpower requirements are underestimated.
- Modeling data were only minimally accurate.

- LCOM scenarios do not adequately represent the current environment under which maintainers must operate.
- Analysis does not account for on-the-job training (OJT) or experience mix.
- Maintenance policies do not reflect reality.
- Manpower availability is averaged across the entire Air Force.
- OJT should be an explicit requirement.
- Overtime should be limited either by policy or by targeted increases in authorizations.
- Greater specificity should be injected into man-hour availability rules.

Comparing the Costs of DoD Military and Civil Service Personnel

Authors: Susan B. Gates and Albert A. Robbert
Publisher: RAND, National Defense Research Institute
Date: 1998
For: Office of the Secretary of Defense

Purpose/Summary/Abstract

- Determine the best methods by which to calculate costs and benefits of military and civilian assignments in certain jobs in DoD.
- Determine the costs of civil service work years and military work years at specific grade levels.
- Determine which assumptions about military and civil service grade distributions and substitution ratios are appropriate for comparing the costs of military and civil service personnel.
- Specifically offer cost analyses in order to compare civilian to military workforce costs.

Methodological Approach

- First determine the cost of an incremental work year by Service and pay grade (cost analysis).

- Focus on the elements of cost that differ between civil service and military personnel.
- Examine how sensitive approaches to substitution analysis are to changes in assumptions.
- Determine whether the traditional approach to substitution analysis or a new approach described in the report most accurately reflects the military personnel management and budgeting process.

Results and Recommendations

- The relative cost of military and civil service personnel depends crucially on how the substitution occurs.
- Civilianization can produce cost savings under many, but not all, circumstances.
- The Office of the Secretary of Defense (OSD) should modify its current guidance on military and civil service position assignments.
- Guidance should specify that assignment decisions be predicted on military necessity, cost, and career-progression opportunities.

Personnel Savings in Competitively Sourced DoD Activities: Are They Real? Will They Last?

Authors:	Susan B. Gates and Albert A. Robbert
Publisher:	RAND, National Defense Research Institute
Date:	2000
For:	Office of the Deputy Assistant Secretary of Defense for Civilian Personnel Policy

Purpose/Summary/Abstract

- The purpose of the study was to develop a better understanding of the sources of efficiency improvement generated through the A-76 process, how those improvements are achieved, and whether they could be achieved outside of the A-76 competition.
- The study set about to answer four questions:
  - How substantial are the projected personnel cost savings?

  - How are the projected personnel cost savings achieved?
  - Are those savings real and enduring?
  - Could the personnel cost savings be achieved outside of the A-76 process?
- The study based the comparison of military and civilian personnel on savings.

Methodological Approach

- Conducted a series of detailed case studies of recently completed and implemented A-76 competitions, which involved document reviews of the Performance Work Statements (PWSs), Most Efficient Organizations (MEOs), and contract files.
- Specifically gathered data from before the A-76 competitions and after, in order to compare.

Results and Recommendations

- The study recommended that OSD, Military Departments, and Defense Agencies provide more positive incentives to local commanders and managers to undertake efficiency improvement measures.
- Negative incentives to efficiency-enhancing changes, such as arbitrary budget cuts imposed on installations and manning policies, should be eliminated or reduced.
- Better information (for high-level decisionmaking) requires precise definitions of such terms as *baseline cost* and *cost savings* that are consistent across installations and Services.
- The development of these definitions must include consideration of whether they capture the total cost of an activity to DoD.

An Integrative Modeling Approach for Managing the Total Defense Labor Force

Authors: Adele R. Palmer and C. Peter Rydell
Publisher: RAND, National Defense Research Institute and Project AIR FORCE

Date: 1989
For: OSD and the U.S. Air Force

Purpose/Summary/Abstract

- To introduce the Total Force Management (TFM) modeling approach to evaluating the cost effectiveness of DoD manpower decisions in a total force management context, simultaneously recognizing the roles of the active, reserve, and civilian workforces in achieving both peacetime and wartime operating goals.
- To determine the salient relationships between wartime and peacetime manpower roles and between military and civilian manpower utilization—and how these relationships can be integrated in a manpower management model.

Methodological Approach

- Create a linear programming model that incorporates the following features:
  - Cost effectiveness
  - The link between wartime capability goals and the costs of maintaining inventories during peacetime
  - The understanding that different areas of the DoD endeavor have different combinations of wartime and peacetime capability goals
  - The links among different categories of manpower (AC, RC, and civilian) that result from overlapping capacities to contribute to peacetime performance and wartime capability
  - The value of a worker during both peacetime and wartime.

Results and Recommendations

- Manning decisions based on a total force analysis can differ from those recommended by a conventional two-way analysis (comparing only active and reserve or active and civilian).
- This model supports straightforward general guidelines for choosing different combinations of personnel (AC, RC, and civilian).
- The use of this system could conflict with some current DoD guidelines.

Developing Cost-Effectiveness Guidelines for Managing Personnel Resources in a Total Force Context

Authors: C. Peter Rydell, Adele R. Palmer, and David J. Osbaldeston
Publisher: RAND, National Defense Research Institute
Date: 1991
For: Assistant Secretary of Defense (Force Management and Personnel)

Purpose/Summary/Abstract

- Continue the models and methods developed in the previous study on TFM, to determine the most cost-effective mix of active, reserve, and civilian personnel in manning defense activities.
- Determine whether the previous study was sensitive to the availability of civilians for wartime work.

Methodological Approach

- Showed how the findings from the TFM model can be used to develop guidelines for manning various types of defense activities.
- Modeled personnel management programs that use personnel in more than one activity, e.g.,
  - personnel employed in one fashion during peacetime and in another during wartime
  - personnel used in one activity for part of their careers and in another later in their careers
  - personnel who are relocated between overseas and shipboard activities and U.S. or shore-based activities.
- Used the Part of Force (POF) model developed in the previous study to evaluate labor costs and capabilities and select a personnel force structure that minimizes either aggregate costs or military personnel costs.
- Compared two alternative sets of parameters, first recreating the previous analysis, then expanding the model for this analysis.
- Developed "cost effectiveness criteria."

- Compared existing guidance and cost-minimizing management.

Results and Recommendations

- Even if using civilians is less costly than using active personnel and even if civilians are fully available for wartime work, costs may nevertheless be saved by replacing some civilians with active personnel under a mobilization program.
- Even if civilians are available for both peacetime and wartime work in a nondeployable activity, costs can be saved by replacing them with active personnel rotating from deployable activities elsewhere.

Military Personnel: Military Departments Need to Ensure That Full Costs of Converting Military Health Care Positions to Civilian Positions Are Reported to Congress

Publisher: U.S. Government Accountability Office
Date: 2006
For: Report to congressional committees

Purpose/Summary/Abstract

- To study the military departments' plans and progress and the potential effects on the Defense Health Program (DHP) of converting military health care positions to civilian positions and the departments' experiences in filling these converted positions with civilians.
- To determine the potential effects on the DHP of converting military health care positions to civilian positions.

Methodological Approach

- Reviewed the pertinent documents, reports, and other information related to the conversion of military health care positions to federal civilian or contract positions.
- Conducted interviews with cognizant officials in the TRICARE Management Activity.

- Analyzed, by geographical area, the data collected to identify the characteristics of officials' experiences in filling the federal civilian or contract position and identify reasons for difficulties in filling positions, if any.
- Gave specific attention to
  - the potential effects of the conversions on medical readiness
  - the potential effects of the conversions on the quality of care
  - the effects on access to care
  - the potential effect of the conversions on the cost of defense health care to DoD.

Results and Recommendations

- Coordinate the development of Services' congressional certifications for health care conversions with the Office of Program Analysis and Evaluation to consider the full cost for military personnel and for federal civilian or contract replacement personnel in assessing whether anticipated costs to hire civilian replacement personnel will increase costs to DoD for defense health care.
- Address, in the Services' congressional certifications for military health care conversions, the extent to which total projected costs for hiring federal civilian or contract personnel include actual compensation costs for completed hires and anticipated compensation costs for future hires.

Force Structure: Assessments of Navy Reserve Manpower Requirements Need to Consider the Most Cost-Effective Mix of Active and Reserve Manpower to Meet Mission Needs

Publisher: U.S. Government Accountability Office
Date: 2005
For: Report to congressional committees

Purpose/Summary/Abstract

- To determine the criteria and process the Navy uses to conduct its zero-based review of reserve manpower requirements and what, if any, limitations affect the Navy's analyses and implementation plans.
- To determine how the recommendations from the zero-based review affect the reserve's manpower, funding, and command and control relationship with the active force.

Methodological Approach

- Examined the results of the reviews of ten Navy activities and visited the Naval Air Forces Command and four other selected activities to assess the zero-based review process at the activity level and obtain detailed information about recommended reserve manpower changes.
- Analyzed the guidance and expectations the Chief of Naval Operations provided to the Fleet Forces Command concerning the zero-based review and those of the Fleet Forces Command to the naval activities concerning
  - the criteria used to determine the required reserve manpower
  - how the activities should report their review results to the Fleet Forces Command
  - the review and validation process for the results reached during the zero-based review
  - plans for implementing the zero-based review results.

Results and Recommendations

- The zero-based review is a critical element in helping the Navy achieve its desire to reduce manpower costs and move toward a more affordable total force.
- The use of capability gaps in the active force as the means to determine reserve manpower requirements was too narrow and failed to consider manpower cost-effectiveness as directed by DoD guidance; this approach did not provide assurance that the Navy will have the most cost-effective mix of active and reserve forces in the future.

Military Personnel: DoD Needs to Conduct a Data–Driven Analysis of Active Military Personnel Levels Required to Implement the Defense Strategy

Publisher: U.S. Government Accountability Office
Date: 2005
For: Report to congressional committees

Purpose/Summary/Abstract

- To assess the extent to which
  - OSD has conducted a data-based analysis of active military personnel needed to implement the national defense strategy
  - OSD has a plan for making more efficient use of active military personnel and evaluating the plan's results.

Methodological Approach

- Identified and examined relevant laws, presidential documents, and DoD guidance, reports, and analyses related to active military personnel and the defense strategy.
- Examined the Services' guidance on processes for determining personnel requirements for the total force to identify the methodologies, time frames, and organizations involved in these processes.
- Examined guidance on the Services' processes for allocating manpower resources.

Results and Recommendations

- OSD does not review the Services' requirements processes and their results on a systematic basis to ensure that decisions about the levels of active personnel are driven by data that establish clear links between personnel levels and capabilities needed to achieve the goals of the defense strategy
- Recommends that OSD
  - establish an OSD-led, systematic approach to assess the levels of active military personnel needed to execute the defense strat-

egy as part of the next quadrennial review and report its analysis and conclusions to Congress
- develop a plan to manage and evaluate DoD's initiatives to assign a greater portion of active military personnel to warfighting duties.

Birth of a Profession: Four Decades of Military Cost Analysis

Author: Paul G. Hough
Publisher: RAND
Date: 1989

Purpose/Summary/Abstract

- To trace the progress and growth of cost analysis as a discipline from the 1950s to the present as a qualitative history and from a quantitative standpoint.
- To demonstrate how the introductions of new concepts and changes in the role of cost analysis were often results of political influences, changing economic fortunes and personalities, inside and outside DoD.

Methodological Approach

- This report was purely descriptive and historical in nature.

Results and Recommendations

- Over the past four decades, military autonomy in acquisition, among other areas, has eroded.
- The defense budget has been subject to far greater scrutiny due to competition among the Services and between DoD and other national priorities.

Inside the Black Box: Assessing the Navy's Manpower Requirements Process

Authors: Carol S. Moore et al.
Publisher: Center for Naval Analyses
Date: 2002

Purpose/Summary/Abstract

- To determine answers to the following questions:
  - Is it possible to reduce shipboard manning while maintaining operational standards?
  - What can a requirements process achieve? To what extent do Navy business practices support or undermine those processes?
  - What are the main drivers of manpower requirements? Do those drivers make sense?
  - How do private companies determine requirements? Might these practices be of value to the Navy?

Methodological Approach

- Focused on existing ships—legacy platforms—as opposed to designs for the future.
- Interviews conducted with Navy officials and five private-sector companies from the manufacturing, shipping, and service industries.
- Primarily descriptive.

Results and Recommendations

- The Navy can significantly improve its manpower requirements process for legacy platforms by taking steps to
  - make the costs (and benefits) of billets more visible and integrate them into the requirements process
  - shift the focus from workload validation toward innovation and improvement

– charge an agent or organization with identifying areas for manpower savings, through methodological, technological, or organizational changes.

The Navy Manpower Requirements System

Author: Peter F. Kostiuk
Publisher: Center for Naval Analyses
Date: August 1987

Purpose/Summary/Abstract

- Described and evaluated the process used by the Navy to set, implement, and execute manpower requirements (circa late 1980s).
- Key problem areas identified include the following:
  - Personnel inventory and requirements databases are not integrated.
  - Manpower requirements for sealift manning are not included in the Navy's mobilization requirements.
  - Peacetime-only billets are not identified.
- Concluded that requirements methodologies are reasonably sound for ship and squadron requirements, but less so for the shore establishment.
- Also concluded that there is insufficient linkage between new weapon system and platform development and manpower requirements.

Methodological Approach

- Not explicitly discussed in the report, but most likely a combination of literature and document reviews, interviews, and other analyses of the manpower requirements process.

Results and Recommendations

- Include Selected Reserve authorizations in the Navy Manpower Data Accounting System.

- Develop a database to track both authorizations and personnel filling billets.
- Evaluate the feasibility and desirability of creating a flexible personnel account within the Selected Reserve to provide personnel in the event of a national emergency.

Operational Medical Manpower: Profiles and Requirement Determination Processes

Authors: Flora Tsui and Theresa Kimble
Publisher: Center for Naval Analyses
Date: February 2001

Purpose/Summary/Abstract

- Study's purpose was to support the N81 M&P IWAR (Manpower and Personnel Integrated Warfare Architecture) 2000 initiative to align Navy operational capabilities with requirements.
- Contains a detailed profile of Navy and Marine Corps operational medical billets. Also discusses the manpower requirements process for these billets in one chapter. Reviews enlisted and officer requirements processes and includes key process steps; diagrams these in flow charts. Navy enlisted requirements are based on workloads; Navy officers on other demands (e.g., command authority, special skills and knowledge).

Methodological Approach

- Analyzed BuPers (Naval Bureau of Personnel) data on operational medical billets in the Navy from 1990 to 2004 (projected).
- Quantified and profiled operational medical billets for both Navy fleet and Fleet Marine Forces (FMF).
- Surveyed literature and documentation on medical manpower requirements determination processes; also conducted site visits and interviews to understand medical manpower requirements processes to supplement documentation and literature review.

Results and Recommendations

- Concludes that the Navy manpower requirements process is much more formal and analytical than the Marine Corps process. The Marines tend to use historical rules for determining medical manpower requirements.
- Recommends a validation of the Navy process or model, and a more formal process or model for the Marine Corps.
- Also recommends that casualty estimates be considered in manpower requirements models.

Manpower Requirements Determination In the Institutional Army

Author: James A. Cooke
Publisher: U.S. Army War College
Date: February 2003

Purpose/Summary/Abstract

- Examined the history of the institutional Army's workload-based manpower requirements determination program in an attempt to identify key problem areas and offer recommendations to make the program more responsive to the Army's strategic decision-making process.

Methodological Approach

- Not explicitly discussed in the report, but probably a literature and document review of Army manpower requirements processes.
- Historical analysis of the institutional Army's manpower requirements process.

Results and Recommendations

- Three major recommendations:
  - "Hold the course"—the TDA Army should stop changing direction with respect to its manpower requirements determination program and settle on a consistent process.

- Centralize the organization of the program and establish authority and responsibility for its oversight and operation.
- Do a better job of linking (declining) resources with (expanding) missions.

Is NAVSO [United States Navy Forces, Southern Command] Organized and Staffed to Do Its Job?

Authors: Karen D. Smith et al.
Publisher: Center for Naval Analyses
Date: January 2002

Purpose/Summary/Abstract

- Studied the newly established NAVSO component command organization and manning levels to determine whether its organization structure and manning levels are appropriate.

Methodological Approach

- Conducted benchmarking of manning at comparable past and current commands.
- Conducted historical analysis of southern command organizations.
- Examined doctrinal and mission requirements.
- Assessed the role of information technology in manning requirements.

Results and Recommendations

- Concluded that NAVSO manning levels were inadequate; NAVSO has the smallest staff of all the Navy component commands.
- Recommendations related to manpower are highly specific and include the following:
  - Increase manning in the small N3 department.
  - Provide an N8 (one O-6 and one civilian).

- Add a liaison officer to the Commander in Chief, Atlantic Fleet (USN 2nd Fleet).
- Provide staff for liaison with government of Puerto Rico.

Analysis of Submarine Tender Manning Issues

Authors: Monica F. Hayes and Alan J. Marcus
Publisher: Center for Naval Analyses
Date: January 1988

Purpose/Summary/Abstract

- Presented a brief analysis of the personnel and requirements issues involved in submarine Intermediate Maintenance Activities (IMAs).
- Investigated whether submarine tender workloads are increasing and manning levels are adequate.

Methodological Approach

- Examined longitudinal enlisted personnel data for retention analysis.
- Compared manning levels on submarine tenders with those on other ships, using actual manning levels versus authorized billets.
- Conducted site visits and interviews.
- Studied pay of submarine tender personnel versus other ship personnel.
- Studied workloads by reviewing maintenance data.

Results and Recommendations

- Submarine tenders are receiving their fair share of available assets (i.e., personnel).
- Authors could not determine whether manpower requirements were adequate, given a lack of information on submarine maintenance activities and workloads.

Navy Actions Needed to Optimize Ship Crew Size and Reduce Total Ownership Costs

Authors: N/A
Publisher: U.S. Government Accountability Office
Date: June 2003

Purpose/Summary/Abstract

- GAO was asked to evaluate the Navy's progress at optimizing ship crew size for four types of ships being developed and acquired.
- The Navy's use of human systems engineering principles and crew size reduction goals varied significantly across the four types of ships.

Methodological Approach

- Analyzed ship crewing documents and human systems integration plans, as well as acquisition and procurement documents.
- Interviewed DoD staff, contractors, and human systems engineering experts.

Results and Recommendations

- GAO recommended that the Navy
  - use human systems engineering principles to optimize ship crew size
  - clearly define the human systems integration certification standards for new ships
  - formally establish a process to examine and facilitate the adoption of labor-saving technologies and best practices across Navy systems.

Comparative Analysis of Navy and Marine Corps Planning, Programming, Budgeting, and Execution Systems from a Manpower Perspective

Authors: John C. Barry and Paul L. Gillikin

Publisher: Naval Postgraduate School (thesis)
Date: March 2005

Purpose/Summary/Abstract

- Conducted a comparative analysis of the organizational and process differences between Navy and Marine Corps manpower planning, budgeting, and execution.
- Found that the Navy has functions consolidated in the N1 office, while the Marine Corps splits them between two offices.

Methodological Approach

- Used the Organizational Systems Framework to analyze Navy and Marine Corps manpower organizations and processes.
- Conducted interviews with key stakeholders.

Results and Recommendations

- Recommends that manpower requirements determination and budgetary authority be consolidated in one office for the Marine Corps.

A Parametric Cost Model for Estimating Operating and Support Costs of U.S. Navy (Non-Nuclear) Surface Ships

Author: James M. Brandt
Publisher: Naval Postgraduate School (thesis)
Date: June 1999

Purpose/Summary/Abstract

- Formulated a parametric cost model to be used in determining annual operating and support costs of non-nuclear surface ships based on known or assumed physical and manpower characteristics.

Methodological Approach

- Used Naval Center for Cost Analysis (NCCA) "VAMOSC" data.
- Used standard regression and statistical analysis (OLS and ANOVA) to develop cost relationships of ship displacement, length, and manpower.

Results and Recommendations

- Develops a single variable predictive cost model; finds significant positive relationships between operations and support (O&S) costs and ship displacement, length, and manpower.
- Manpower is treated as an exogenous independent variable; there is no analysis of the manpower requirements process or how such a process can be fiscally informed.

Littoral Combat Ship (LCS) Manpower Requirements Analysis

Author: Thaveephone Douangaphaivong
Publisher: Naval Postgraduate School (thesis)
Date: December 2004

Purpose/Summary/Abstract

- Argued that current directives for LCS manning (approximately 75 manpower requirements) cannot be obtained without major paradigm shifts. "Smart Ship" and other efficiency initiatives will not be enough to reduce crew size to target levels.

Methodological Approach

- Apparently used a linear programming approach to minimize ship crew size.
- Estimated minimum crew required to staff classes of LCSs.

Results and Recommendations

- Estimated annual manpower savings of $80 million to $110 million under certain conditions; this is the only fiscal element of the study.

The Cost and Benefits of Reduced Manning for U.S. Naval Combatants

Author: Matthew G. Fleming
Publisher: Naval Postgraduate School (thesis)
Date: March 1997

Purpose/Summary/Abstract

- To conduct a cost benefit analysis of "Smart Ship," the initiative to reduce manpower and life -cycle costs.

Methodological Approach

- Used cost-benefit analysis.
- Used previous studies of manpower, readiness, and labor productivity (literature review).

Results and Recommendations

- Found that a 0.54 percent reduction in the total budget of the Department of the Navy was possible through Smart Ship but that the initiative might be "risky and imprudent" for purely cost-saving reasons.

Restructuring the United States Navy Chaplain Corps

Author: Kenneth G. Harris
Publisher: Naval Postgraduate School (thesis)
Date: September 2005

Purpose/Summary/Abstract

- Investigated (1) whether the chaplain function should necessarily be performed by a commissioned officer and (2) whether there is a potential savings from eliminating or outsourcing the function.

Methodological Approach

- Not a rigorously quantitative study; mainly a literature review supplemented with interviews and informal surveys.

Results and Recommendations

- Estimates that $69 million in potential savings from divestiture of most shipboard and shore-based chaplain positions.
- Outsourcing would save approximately $37.5 million.
- Outsourcing is said to be the inferior approach.

The Shipbuilding and Force Structure Analysis Tool: A User's Guide

Authors: Mark V. Arena, John F. Schank, and Megan Abbott
Publisher: RAND, National Defense Research Institute
Date: 2004

Purpose/Summary/Abstract

- Describes the result of efforts to implement an integrated architecture to analyze the industrial base elements involved in the Navy's future force structure.
- The purpose of the analysis tool is to assist OSD and the Navy in addressing difficult naval ship-related questions. The tool involves four models:
  - force transition
  - industrial base
  - O&S
  - financial adjustments and assumptions.

Methodological Approach

- Cost modeling.

Results and Recommendations

- The O&S model component takes force transition model outputs (e.g., number and type of ships) and uses four inputs:
  - O&S costs by class and age
  - annual personnel costs
  - maintenance labor rates
  - operating plan, with operational cost as its output.
- Manpower requirements are a given.

Flag Pole Service Delivery Study—METOC [Meteorological and Oceanographic] Services: Briefing to the N1—5 January 2004

Authors: N/A
Publisher: LMI
Date: January 5, 2004

Purpose/Summary/Abstract

- To research and analyze current methods for determining manpower in the Navy.
- To find areas of manpower determination that could be streamlined to save money for the Navy.
- To cut back on manpower.

Methodological Approach

- 90-day independent study composed of various smaller studies
- Zero-based reviews
- Service delivery reviews
- Area analyses
- Progression analyses
- Interviews

- Researching Inspector General reports and guidance set forth by various Navy departments.

Results and Recommendations

- Outsource billets for 25 percent of Fleet Numerical Meteorology and Oceanography Center (FNMOC) and the Naval Oceanographic Office (NAVO).
- Convert FNMOC and NAVO production centers to civilian billets.
- Consolidate regional forecasting centers into one area and forecasting support to two areas.
- Reduce the deployed footprint by redesigning deployment concept.
- Reduce staff footprint where operational return on investment is less clear.

DARPA [Defense Advanced Research Projects Agency] Carrier Manpower Reduction Study

Authors: David K. Hegland and Michael F. Wanjon
Publisher: Whitney, Bradley, and Brown
Date: June 2006

Purpose/Summary/Abstract

- To develop an analytical methodology to assess the suitability and risk of carrier manpower reduction initiatives.
- To identify technologies and organizational initiatives to reduce carrier manpower by 1,500 billets and enable a 900-person aircraft carrier.

Methodological Approach

- Analyzed the current carrier manpower standard
- Studied allied navies, commercial ship builders, and operators
- Identified key positions and requirements "billet drivers"

- Built metrics to compare costs, risks, feasibility, and operational, quality-of-life, and manpower impacts
- Compared the similar functions between the different navies and corporate entities and made recommendations.

Results and Recommendations

- The method produced results that were very specific to the carrier mission.
- The billet reduction of 1,500 set forth in the objectives is achievable.
- Manpower requirements process needs more rigor.
- Current Navy manpower models are not suited for identifying and assessing large billet reductions.
- Sea Warrior will require reassessment of billet saving opportunities.
- Culture and tradition are large impediments to crew reduction.
- Navy should adopt the Enterprise Model or create a single manpower reduction advocate to execute force-wide manpower reduction efforts.
- DARPA should adopt high-potential advanced technology areas as candidates for future study and development.

Skill Mix, Experience, and Readiness

Author: Stanley A. Horowitz
Publisher: Center for Naval Analyses
Date: October 1983

Purpose/Summary/Abstract

- The purpose of the study was "to argue that we can do better" at designing a military personnel system that takes into account the contribution to readiness of different kinds of personnel (in terms of skills and experience).
- The study attempted to answer three broad questions:

- Can it be shown that the experience and pay grade mix of military personnel generally affects the military performance of units?
- Can the magnitude of the effects be determined?
- How should this sort of information influence policy?

Methodological Approach

- Reviews two earlier studies by the Center for Naval Analyses that relate experience to unit performance: *The Characteristics of Naval Personnel and Personnel Performance,* by Stanley Horowitz and Allan Sherman (1977), and *Personnel Substitution and Navy Aviation Readiness,* by Alan Marcus (1982). Horowitz and Sherman demonstrate that measures correlated with experience (e.g., pay grade, length of service, and prior sea experience) increase readiness (measured by mission degrading downtime of ships). Marcus considers substitution of personnel with differing productivity and cost, using A-7 squadron sortie data.
- Summarizes the results of the two studies, cites others relating accession and retention rates to bonuses, and makes general recommendations for policy.

Results and Recommendations:

- "The relationship between experience and military performance can be quantified, and we should take advantage of it." (Page 10)
- Requirements should be set with consideration of the value marginal product of labor of military personnel, and the compensation system should be designed accordingly.
- "All evidence indicates that we'd be better off with a more senior force. We should take fewer people into the Navy and do a better job of keeping those we take." (Page 10)
- The Navy should pay more for experience.

Table A.1 groups the studies in this appendix according to the taxonomy described in Table 3.1.

Table A.1
Summary of Studies

	Aspect									
Study	Fiscally Informed	Functional	Organiza-tional	Occupa-tional	Service	Descriptive	Prescriptive	Integrative	External	Internal
Rattelman et al., 2001	x	x			x	x	x	x	x	
GAO, March 1986	x	x				x	x	x	x	
Dahlman et al., 2002		x			x	x	x	x	x	
Gates and Robbert, 1998	x		x	x			x	x	x	
Gates and Robbert, 2000	x	x		x			x	x	x	
Palmer and Rydell, 1989	x		x				x	x	x	
Rydell et al., 1991	x			x			x	x	x	
GAO, 2006	x	x		x		x	x		x	
GAO, 2005	x		x		x	x	x		x	

Table A.1—Continued

Study	Aspect								
	Fiscally Informed	Functional	Organiza-tional	Occupa-tional	Service	Descriptive	Prescriptive	Integrative	External	Internal
GAO, 2005		x	x				x		x	
Hough, 1989	x	x							x	
Moore et al., 2002	x		x		x	x	x	x	x	
Kostiuk, 1987					x	x	x		x	
Tsui and Kimble, 2001	x					x	x		x	
Cooke, 2003					x	x	x			x
Smith et al., 2002			x		x		x		x	
Hayes and Marcus, 1988		x			x		x		x	
GAO, 2003	x				x		x		x	

Table A.1—Continued

Study	Aspect									
	Fiscally Informed	Functional	Organizational	Occupational	Service	Descriptive	Prescriptive	Integrative	External	Internal
Barry and Gillikin, 2005		x	x			x	x	x	x	
Brandt, 1999		x			x				x	
Naval Postgrad. School, 2004	x				x		x		x	
Fleming, 1997	x				x		x		x	
Harris, 2005	x	x							x	
Arena, Schank, and Abbott, 2004	x	x			x				x	x
LMI, 2004	x			x	x		x		x	
Hegland and Wanjon, 2006			x		x		x		x	

Table A.1—Continued

Study	Aspect									
	Fiscally Informed	Functional	Organiza-tional	Occupa-tional	Service	Descriptive	Prescriptive	Integrative	External	Internal
Horowitz, 1983	x				x	x	x		x	

NOTE:

Fiscally informed = Study bases its findings and recommendations on fiscal information.

Functional = Study focuses on one function across several departments.

Organizational = Study focuses on one organization with several functions.

Occupational = Study focuses on particular functions that each department possesses.

Service = Study focuses primarily on one Service.

Descriptive = Study describes the current methods for determining manpower requirement.

Prescriptive = Study prescribes methods by which manpower determinations might be improved.

Integrative = Study breaks the subjects down, describing and prescribing methods for each components.

External = Study was performed by a party external to the subject organization.

Internal = Study was performed by a party internal to the subject organization.

Bibliography

Allison, Graham, and Phillip Zelikow, *Essence of Decision*, 2nd ed., New York: Longman, 1999.

Aspin, Les, *The Bottom-Up Review: Forces for a New Era,* Washington, D.C.: U.S. Government Printing Office, September 1993.

Arena, Mark V., John F. Schank, and Megan Abbott, *The Shipbuilding and Force Structure Analysis Tool: A User's Guide,* Santa Monica, Calif.: RAND Corporation, MR-1743-NAVY, 2004. As of February 13, 2008: http://www.rand.org/pubs/monograph_reports/MR1743/

Barry, John C., and Paul L. Gillikin, *Comparative Analysis of Navy and Marine Corps Planning, Programming, Budgeting, and Execution Systems from a Manpower Perspective*, Monterey, Calif.: Naval Postgraduate School, A195234, March 2005.

Brandt, James M., *A Parametric Cost Model for Estimating Operating and Support Costs of U.S. Navy (Non-Nuclear) Surface Ships*, Monterey, Calif.: Naval Postgraduate School, A935363, June 1999.

Cooke, James A., *Manpower Requirements Determination in the Institutional Army,* Carlisle Barracks, Pa.: U.S. Army War College, ADA414538, February 2003.

Dahlman, Carl J., Robert Kerchner, and David E. Thaler, *Setting Requirements for Maintenance Manpower in the U.S. Air Force*, Santa Monica, Calif.: RAND Corporation, MR-1436-AF, 2002. As of February 13, 2008: http://www.rand.org/pubs/monograph_reports/MR1436/

Defense Manpower Commission, *Defense Manpower: The Keystone of National Security: Report to the President and the Congress,* Washington, D.C., April 1976.

DoD—*See* U.S. Department of Defense.

Douangaphaivong, Thaveephone, *Littoral Combat Ship (LCS) Manpower Requirements Analysis*, Monterey, Calif.: Naval Postgraduate School, A987924, December 2004.

Emmerichs, Robert M., Cheryl Y. Marcum, and Albert A. Robbert, *An Operational Process for Workforce Planning*, Santa Monica, Calif.: RAND

Corporation, MR-1684/1-OSD, 2004. As of February 13, 2008:
http://www.rand.org/pubs/monograph_reports/MR1684.1/

Fleming, Matthew G., *The Cost and Benefits of Reduced Manning for U.S. Naval Combatants*, Monterey, Calif.: Naval Postgraduate School, A354333, March 1997.

GAO—*See* U.S. Government Accountability Office (prior to 2004, U.S. General Accounting Office)

Gates, Susan M., Christine Eibner, and Edward G. Keating, *Civilian Workforce Planning in the Department of Defense: Different Levels, Different Roles,* Santa Monica, Calif.: RAND Corporation, MG-449-OSD, 2006. As of February 13, 2008:
http://www.rand.org/pubs/monographs/MG449/

Gates, Susan M., and Albert A. Robbert, *Comparing the Costs of DoD Military and Civil Service Personnel*, Santa Monica, Calif.: RAND Corporation, MR-980-OSD, 1998. As of February 13, 2008:
http://www.rand.org/pubs/monograph_reports/MR980/

———, *Personnel Savings in Competitively Sourced DoD Activities: Are They Real? Will They Last?* Santa Monica, Calif.: RAND Corporation, MR-1117-OSD, 2000. As of February 13, 2008:
http://www.rand.org/pubs/monograph_reports/MR1117/

Harris, Kenneth G., *Restructuring the United States Navy Chaplain Corps,* Monterey, Calif.: Naval Postgraduate School, September 2005.

Hatch, William D. II, Arthur J. Ohanian, and Cary A. Simon, *Ship's Officer Staffing Guide: Report of Findings and Recommendations*, NPS-GSBPP-03-005, Monterey, Calif.: Naval Postgraduate School, 2003.

Hayes, Monica F., and Alan J. Marcus, *Analysis of Submarine Tender Manning Issues*, Alexandria, Va.: Center for Naval Analyses, CRM-87-203, January 1988.

Hegland, David K., and Michael F. Wanjon, *DARPA Carrier Manpower Reduction Study*, Vienna, Va.: Whitney, Bradley and Brown, June, 2006.

Horowitz, Stanley A., *Skill Mix, Experience, and Readiness*, Alexandria, Va.: Center for Naval Analyses, October 1983.

Kirby, Sheila Nataraj, and Harry J. Thie, *Enlisted Personnel Management: A Historical Perspective*, Santa Monica, Calif.: RAND Corporation, MR-755-OSD, 1996. As of February 13, 2008:
http://www.rand.org/pubs/monograph_reports/MR755/

Hough, Paul G., *Birth of a Profession: Four Decades of Military Cost Analysis,* Santa Monica, Calif.: RAND Corporation, P-7539, August 1989. As of March 18, 2008:
http://www.rand.org/pubs/papers/P7539/

Kostiuk, Peter F., *The Navy Manpower Requirements System,* Alexandria, Va.: Center for Naval Analyses, CRM-87-114, August 1987.

Larson, Eric V., David T. Orletsky, and Kristin Leuschner, *Defense Planning in a Decade of Change: Lessons from the Base Force, Bottom-Up Review, and Quadrennial Defense Review,* Santa Monica, Calif.: RAND Corporation, MR-1387, 2001. As of February 13, 2008:
http://www.rand.org/pubs/monograph_reports/MR1387/

LMI, *"Flag Pole" Service Delivery Study–METOC Services: Briefing to the N1,* Washington, D.C.: LMI, January 5, 2004.

March, James G., and Herbert A Simon, *Organizations,* New York: John Wiley and Sons, 1963.

Moore, Carol S., and Anita U. Hattiangadi, with G. Thomas Sicilia and James L. Gasch, *Inside the Black Box: Assessing the Navy's Manpower Requirements Process,* Alexandria, Va.: Center for Naval Analyses, CRM-D0005206.A2, March 2002.

Morgan, F. J., Leonard V. Scifers, and D. K. Shelton, *Air Reserve Forces Personnel Study,* Vol. IV: *Personnel Shortages and Combat Capability,* Santa Monica, Calif.: RAND Corporation, R-1459-PR, 1974. As of March 19, 2008:
http://www.rand.org/pubs/reports/R1459/

Office of Management and Budget, *Circular A-76, SUBJECT: Performance of Commercial Activities,* May 29, 2003. As of March 10, 2008:
http://www.dla.mil/j-3/a-76/OMBCircularA-76New.html

Palmer, Adele R., and C. Peter Rydell, *An Integrative Modeling Approach for Managing the Total Defense Labor Force,* Santa Monica, Calif.: RAND Corporation, R-3756-OSD/AF, December 1989. As of February 13, 2008:
http://www.rand.org/pubs/reports/R3756/

Public Law 99-433, Department of Defense Reorganization Act, December 12, 1985.

Rakoff, Stuart H., *Report on Army-Navy Workforce Planning Demonstration Symposium,* presented at 6th Annual Navy Workforce Research Conference, March 26, 2006.

Rattelman, Cori, Robert Levy, Neil Carey, and Flora Tsui, *Wartime Medical Requirements: Profiles and Requirement Determination Process,* Alexandria, Va.: Center for Naval Analyses, CAB D0004694.A2, October 2001.

Rostker, Bernard, *Air Reserve Forces Personnel Study*, Vol. I: *The Personnel Structure and Posture of the Air National Guard and the Air Force Reserve,* Santa Monica, Calif.: RAND Corporation, R-1049-PR, 1973. As of March 19, 2008:
http://www.rand.org/pubs/reports/R1049/

———, *Air Reserve Forces Personnel Study*, Vol. III: *Total Force Planning, Personnel Costs, and the Supply of New Reservists,* Santa Monica, Calif.: RAND Corporation, R-1430-PR, 1974. As of March 19, 2008:
http://www.rand.org/pubs/reports/R1430/

Rydell, C. Peter, Adele R. Palmer, and David J. Osbaldeston, *Developing Cost-Effectiveness Guidelines for Managing Personnel Resources in a Total Force Context,* Santa Monica, Calif.: RAND Corporation, R-4005/1-FMP, 1991. As of February 13, 2008:
http://www.rand.org/pubs/reports/R4005.1/

Smith, Karen D., Stephen J. Kim, Patrick H. Roth, Brian E. Walsh, Elizabeth Young, and Kletus S. Lawler, *Is NAVSO Organized and Staffed to Do Its Job?* Alexandria, Va.: Center for Naval Analyses, CRM-D0005057.A1, January 2002.

Tsui, Flora, and Theresa Kimble, *Operational Medical Manpower: Profiles and Requirement Determination Processes,* Alexandria, Va.: Center for Naval Analyses, CRM-D0002906.A2, February 2001.

U.S. Department of Defense, *Report of the Quadrennial Defense Review,* Washington, D.C.: U.S. Government Printing Office, May 1997.

———, *Quadrennial Defense Review Report,* Washington, D.C.: U.S. Government Printing Office, September 30, 2001.

———, Department of Defense Directive 1100.4, *Guidance for Manpower Management,* Washington, D.C.: U.S. Government Printing Office, February 12, 2005. As of February 6, 2008:
www.dtic.mil/whs/directives/corres/pdf/110004p.pdf

———, Department of Defense Instruction 1100.22, *Guidance for Determining Workforce Mix,* Washington, D.C.: U.S. Government Printing Office, September 7, 2006a. As of February 6, 2008:
www.dtic.mil/whs/directives/corres/pdf/110022p.pdf

———, *Quadrennial Defense Review Report,* Washington, D.C.: U.S. Government Printing Office, February 6, 2006b.

U.S. General Accounting Office, *DoD "Total Force Management"—Fact or Rhetoric?* Washington, D.C.: U.S. Government Accountability Office, FPCD-78-82, January 1979.

———, *DoD Manpower: Information on the Accuracy of Defense Manpower Requirements,* Washington, D.C.: U.S. Government Accountability Office, GAO/NSAID-86-87BR, March 26, 1986a.

———, *Navy Manpower: Improved Ship Manpower Document Program Could Reduce Requirements,* Washington, D.C.: U.S. Government Accountability Office, NSIAD-86-49, March 27, 1986b.

———, *Marine Corps Manpower: Improvements Needed in Processes for Determining Manpower Requirements,* Washington, D.C.: U.S. Government Accountability Office, GAO/NSAID-87-102, May 1987a.

———, *Navy Shore Manpower Program: Decision to Decentralize Needs to Be Rethought,* Washington, D.C.: U.S. Government Accountability Office, GAO/NSAID-87-99BR, May 1987b.

———, *Military Officers: Assessment of the 1988 Defense Officer Requirements Study,* Washington, D.C.: U.S. Government Accountability Office, GAO/NSIAD-88-146, April 1988.

———, *Military Personnel: Navy Actions Needed to Optimize Ship Crew Size and Reduce Total Ownership Costs*, Washington, D.C.: U.S. Government Accountability Office, GAO-03-520, June 2003.

———, *Military Personnel: DoD Needs to Conduct a Data-Driven Analysis of Active Military Personnel Levels Required to Implement the Defense Strategy*, Washington, D.C.: U.S. Government Accountability Office, GAO-05-200, February 2005a.

———, *Force Structure: Assessments of Navy Reserve Manpower Requirements Need to Consider the Most Cost-Effective Mix of Active and Reserve Manpower to Meet Mission Needs*, Washington, D.C.: U.S. Government Accountability Office, GAO-06-125, October 2005b.

———, *Military Personnel: Military Departments Need to Ensure That Full Costs of Converting Military Health Care Positions to Civilian Positions Are Reported to Congress,* Washington, D.C.: U.S. Government Accountability Office, GAO-06-642, May 2006.

Vernez, Georges, Albert A. Robbert, Hugh G. Massey, and Kevin Driscoll, *Workforce Planning and Development Processes: A Practical Guide*, Santa Monica, Calif.: RAND Corporation, TR-408-AF, 2007. As of February 13, 2008: http://www.rand.org/pubs/technical_reports/TR408/